Sea Otters

MARIANNE RIEDMAN

MONTEREY BAY AQUARIUM®

Monterey, California

The purpose of the Monterey Bay Aquarium is to stimulate interest, increase knowledge and promote stewardship of Monterey Bay and the world's ocean environment through innovative exhibits, public education and scientific research. One goal lies behind all we do: to help protect the world's oceans.

Acknowledgments I am grateful to the many friends and colleagues who assisted in one way or another with the preparation of this book, especially Nora L. Deans, Judy Rand, Chris Parsons, Steven K. Webster, Roger Luckenbach, Michelle Staedler, Barbara Hrabrich, Susan Kogan, Janey Burger, Alisa Giles, Jack Ames and Jim Estes, as well as the volunteer observers and staff of the aquarium's sea otter research program, and the husbandry staff and volunteers involved in the sea otter rescue and care program. I wish to acknowledge the scientific contributions made by many researchers at the University of California at Santa Cruz, U.S. Fish and Wildlife Service, California Department of Fish and Game, University of Minnesota and the Monterey Bay Aquarium sea otter research program, which I've drawn upon in writing the manuscript. Special thanks are also extended to the Banbury Foundation and Bob and Kate Ernst for their support and encouragement.

This book is dedicated to my mother, Dee Haner, with love and gratitude.

©Published in the United States by the Monterey Bay Aquarium Foundation, 886 Cannery Row, Monterey, CA 93940-1085. http://www.mbayaq.org

Library of Congress Cataloging in Publications Data.
Riedman, Marianne.
Sea otters/Marianne Riedman.

p. cm–(Monterey Bay Aquarium natural history series)
Includes index
ISBN 1-878244-03-5
1. Sea otter. I. Title II. Series
QL737.C25R54 1990
599.74'447-dc20   90-6225 CIP

Photos and Illustration Credits

Cover: Richard Bucich

Back Cover: Jeff Foott (bottom), Frances Thompson (top)

Balthis, Frank S: 11 (top)

Bavendam, Fred: 41 (top), 50

Bucich, Richard: 5 (middle) 22–23, 24, 29 (top), 31, 32-33, 36–37, 40, 41 (bottom), 42 (top), 47, 49 (right), 51 (bottom), 55, 56–57, 57, 58, 60, 64, 67 (top), 68, 69, 76 (bottom), 77 (top), 77 (right), 78, 79

Calhoun, Bob and Clara/ Bruce Coleman Inc.: 19

Caudle, Ann: 39 (top middle), 44 (bottom right)

Davis, John: 44 (top)

Dawson, Tony: 11 (bottom)

Ellis, Gerry: 72

Foott, Jeff: 1, 5 (bottom),6–7,7 (top left), 17, 25 (top), 27 (left), 28–29, 30 (top), 37 (top), 38 (bottom left), 43, 46, 51 (top), 53 (top), 54, 61, 63 (top), 64–65, 67 (top), 75, 77 (bottom left)

Garst, Warren/Tom Stack & Assoc.: 16 (left)

Gohier, Francois: 22, 23 (top)

Gotshall, Daniel W.: 48–49
Hymer, Julie: 12 (bottom), 13, 70–71

Lanting, Frans/Minden Pictures: 53 (middle), 66

McHugh, Tom/National Audubon Collection/Photo Researchers Inc.: 16 (right)

Mangelson, Tom: 18 (top), 20, 76 (top)

Mattison, James: 38 (bottom right)

Mattison, Richard: 39 (bottom)

Monterey Bay Aquarium: 14, 15, 21, 26 (left), 27 (right), 45, 62, 63 (middle, bottom left), (top right), 70

Morgan, William L./Pat Hathaway Collection: 9 (bottom)

Nicklin, Flip/Nicklin & Associates: 30 (middle), 34, 59

Thompson, Frances: 38 (top left, middle & right), 39 (top left, top right)

Ward, Kennan: 4, 26 (right), 73

Williams, Rod/Bruce Coleman Inc.: 18 (bottom)

Wu, Norbert: 25 (bottom), 33, 35 (top), 42 (bottom), 52

Managing Editor: Nora L. Deans

Project Editor: Roxane Buck-Ezcurra

Series Design: James Stockton & Associates

Art Director: Ann W. Douden

Book Design: Archetype, Inc.

Printed in Hong Kong on recycled paper through Global Interprint

Contents

"I was taken out in a little boat . . . and there were the California sea lions sitting on the breakwater honking at us, then after about five minutes we came to the kelp beds, those extraordinary seaweed beds that are so long, glossy and thick, and there in these kelp beds were all the sea otters carefully wrapped up as though they were in bed, all lying on their backs in the water with their heads sticking up and their paws together. They looked like a convention of bishops in mud baths in Baden-Baden or somewhere like that. They are quite the most enchanting animals I think I have ever seen."

— Gerald Durrell

What looks like an enchanting and cuddly creature to many of us is actually a highly specialized and truly remarkable aquatic mammal, uniquely adapted for living in a wet, cold and harsh marine world. Yet the same adaptations that allow sea otters to survive in the cold ocean—

luxurious, thick fur and hearty appetites for shellfish—have also made these mammals extremely vulnerable in a human world.

While we still have much to learn about the behavior of sea otters, we've discovered that otters have unique and distinctive personalities, expressed by the foods they prefer, the way they use tools, their tendency to haul out on land, their mothering styles, their movement patterns, their responses to people and even the sounds they make. In this book I focus on sea otters in California, although you'll also read about Alaskan and Russian sea otters.

As biologists spend long hours in the field observing wild otters from birth to adulthood, they can't help but become attached to these intriguing animals. Perhaps you will too, as you read their stories, many told here for the first time.

1

Recovery of Sea Otters

Until the 1700s, sea otters (*Enhydra lutris*) were abundant across the rim of the North Pacific from northern Japan to the Alaska Peninsula and along the Pacific coast of North America to Baja California. They were especially numerous off the Channel Islands of southern California and the central and northern portions of the state. We don't know for certain how many sea otters lived off California, but biologists think that at one time there were 16,000 to 20,000 California sea otters, perhaps as many as 30,000. The worldwide sea otter population probably totaled 150,000 to 300,000 animals.

Hunted for Furs Aboriginal people hunted sea otters for many thousands of years. Coastal North American Indians, northern Aleuts and the Japanese valued otters for their warm fur. In some areas, the Aleuts overexploited otters and substantially reduced their populations. However, it wasn't until the mid-1700s that widespread commercial hunting of sea otters took place, leading to the near-extinction of the species.

The extremely profitable sea otter fur trade began in 1741, when a shipwrecked Russian expedition led by Vitus Bering discovered sea otters on one of the Commander Islands. There was a great demand in Russia, Europe, Japan and especially China for the beautiful and warm otter pelts. The Russians soon claimed Alaska and enslaved the native Aleuts to do most of their hunting. The slow-swimming otters were easy to kill and "innocent as sheep," according to the expedition's naturalist Georg Steller.

Within 50 years, the Russians and their Aleut hunters nearly exterminated the Alaskan otter population, so the fur traders moved south to California, where otters were still abundant. In the late 1700s, American and English hunters joined in, accelerating the decline of the remaining otter population. Otter fur-trading operations, such as the Hudson's Bay Company, gained far-reaching recognition. (The initials HBC were made fun of by some who said they stood for "Here Before Christ" because the Hudson's Bay Company often established settlements before the missionaries.)

By the early 1900s, sea otters were nearly extinct. Only 1,000 to 2,000 otters survived throughout their range. When the International Fur Seal Treaty of 1911 established protection for sea otters, only 13 small otter colonies persisted from the Kamchatka Peninsula south to Mexico. By the 1920s, the sole surviving group of otters south of Alaska was the Point Sur colony, the ancestors of the current population of California sea otters.

Aleut Indians hunted sea otters for thousands of years, as depicted in this painting by Emilie Curtis. But during the 1700s and 1800s, commercial hunters brought sea otters to the brink of extinction.

Impact of the Fur Trade The booming sea otter fur trade in the eighteenth and nineteenth centuries had monumental historical and biological consequences in the North Pacific. Within the first 15 years of the discovery of sea otters, all of the remaining giant Steller sea cows (*Hydrodamalis gigas*)—large kelp-eating marine mammals related to dugongs and manatees—had been killed to provide food for the Russian otter hunters in the Commander and Aleutian islands. Thus, the gentle but tasty sea cow became extinct in the quest for sea otter furs. Because sea cows fed on shallow-water and surface canopy kelps, their absence undoubtedly had a great effect on kelp forest ecosystems. We can only guess about the important ecological relationships that probably existed between sea cows, sea otters and kelp forest communities.

If the Russian explorers hadn't discovered the Commander Island sea otters during Bering's final Alaskan exploration, they probably wouldn't have explored and settled the northwest coast of America. Canada, not the United States, would most likely have acquired Alaska. As it turned out, Secretary of State Seward was able to buy Alaska in 1867 when the Russians lost interest in their acquisition as the sea otters disappeared.

With the severe depletion of sea otters in California, the Russians also lost interest in their settlement at Fort Ross. In the fall of 1841, the Russians sold the Fort Ross settlement to an American named John Sutter, who had set up a sawmill on the American River to raise money to purchase the Russian property. As luck would have it, gold was discovered in 1848 at the Sutter sawmill, catalyzing the 1849 California "gold rush," and dramatically altering the course of American history.

Hundreds of thousands of sea otters once lived along the Pacific coast from northern Japan to Baja California. Although Alaskan and Russian populations have re-colonized much of their former range, the California otter population is recovering more slowly.

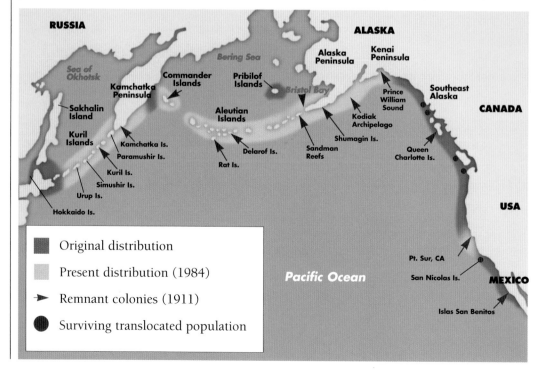

Original distribution

Present distribution (1984)

Remnant colonies (1911)

Surviving translocated population

Slow Recovery Since the early 1900s, the worldwide sea otter population has gradually increased as otters have re-colonized their former range. Today, an estimated 100,000 to 150,000 sea otters live from Russia's Kuril Islands northeast to Prince William Sound, occupying most of their historical range in these areas. Sea otters southeast of Prince William Sound, however, have not made such a successful comeback. Only small groups of Alaskan otters transplanted by biologists now occur off Washington, British Columbia and southeast Alaska. Today, only one native southern sea otter population survives: the sea otters off the central California coast.

The current California population descended from a small group of perhaps 50 otters that lived in seclusion along the isolated and rugged Big Sur coastline. In 1915, 32 otters were observed near Point Sur. The few people who knew about these otters kept their secret and the public did not discover the news until 1938, after the opening of the new coast highway from Monterey to San Simeon. At Bixby Creek bridge, Harold Sharp sighted a small group of sea otters on March 19, 1930, later saying, "I had no premonition that I was verging on a discovery destined to draw an army of spectators from the farthest reaches of the earth . . ."

From the late 1930s until the mid-1970s, the number of California sea otters slowly but steadily increased. The California population has always grown at a rate four to five times slower than the growth rate of other recently established populations in Alaska, perhaps due in part to a higher pup mortality rate in California. This slow but steady increase stopped after the mid-1970s and the otter population even declined in the early 1980s to total only about 1,200 to 1,300 animals.

On April 15, 1938, the public became aware of the sole remaining group of California sea otters living in Bixby Creek Cove along the Big Sur coast. Once thought to be extinct, biologists had first discovered them in 1915 but kept their presence a secret.

What slowed the growth of the California sea otter population during the 1970s to early 1980s? Biologists suspect that many otters drowned accidentally in nearshore gill nets and trammel fishing nets. Because of the frequent drownings, an emergency closure in January 1985 prohibited the use of such fishing nets from Monterey to the Santa Maria River in waters shallower than 90 feet, or 15 fathoms, which is where otters tend to forage. In September 1986, the restrictions were extended to 20 fathoms in certain areas off Big Sur. Currently, the use of gill and trammel nets is prohibited in waters of 30 fathoms or less from Waddell Creek in Santa Cruz County to Point Sal in Santa Barbara County. Naturally, the fishing industry didn't welcome these restrictions. Yet since the closures, scientists have observed far fewer net-drowned otters, and the sea otter population began to expand again.

Surveys made over the past several years show that the California otter population increased at a mean growth rate of about five-and-a-half percent. Yet the 1996 count was low for unknown reasons, and little growth occurred in the previous year.

In 1996, researchers counted 2,278 sea otters, including 1,963 adult and juvenile otters and 315 pups, along the California coast. Because otter census-takers miss about five-and-a-half percent of the otters during a shore-based survey, the estimate for the 1996 California population was about 2,400 otters.

Most California sea otters currently live along about 235 miles of coastline from Point Año Nuevo to Purisima Point, just south of the Santa Maria River in San Luis Obispo County. Although sightings of sea otters outside their established range are rare, otters have been seen as far north as Cape Mendocino and along the southern California coast to northern Baja California.

The California sea otter population has been slowly expanding since 1938.

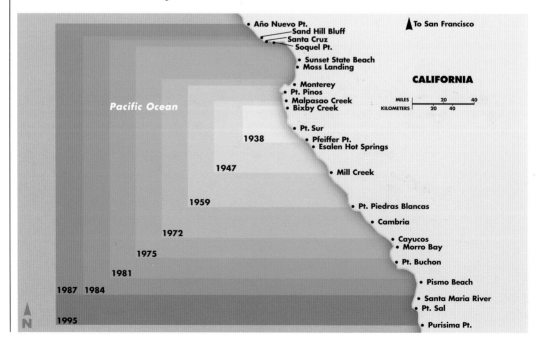

Resource Conflicts Sea otters compete with people for shellfish, leading to conflicts between what's best for otters and what's best for commercial-fishing industries. Most commercial shellfisheries cannot profitably co-exist with sea otters over a long period of time because otters substantially reduce populations of abalones, clams and sea urchins. California's shellfish industries were founded in the early 1900s when otters were scarce. Without otters, the shellfish flourished. Commercial shellfisheries took advantage of this artificial overabundance of large shellfish, especially abalone.

Abalone is a favorite meal for many sea otters, which brings them in conflict with commercial shellfishermen.

Over the past century, shellfish resources have declined, due in part to the increased number of sea otters but also because of overfishing and poor management practices. Careful management is essential to preserve both sea otters and the shellfish industry. Recent advances in mariculture, in which abalone are artificially cultivated, hold much promise. A significant number of restaurant abalone now come from mariculture production.

Conflicts of interest also exist between the California sea otter and the oil and gas industry. Sea otters are extremely sensitive to the effects of oil contamination. A major oil spill could endanger much of the California population. An oil tanker accident, like the *Exxon Valdez* disaster in March 1989, or blowouts of drilling operations, could cause such an oil spill. Hundreds of Alaskan sea otters perished after the *Exxon Valdez* released more than ten million gallons of crude oil into pristine Prince William Sound. The oil and gas industry is therefore subject to various restrictions in their oil exploration activities within the California sea otter's range. Some oil companies, concerned about the possibility of oil spills, have helped to develop sea otter oil spill contingency plans, including methods for cleaning oiled otters. But prevention of spills is the best strategy, since capturing and successfully rehabilitating oiled otters is quite difficult.

Cleaning sea otters contaminated by oil, like this tranquilized otter at the Valdez Otter Rescue Center in Alaska, involves scrubbing with dishwashing detergent and repeated rinsing to get rid of any trace of the toxic oil.

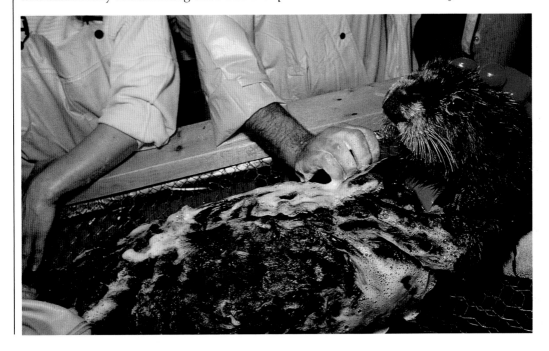

In order to prevent the potential extinction of the small California sea otter population should a catastrophic oil spill occur, a group of sea otters was moved from the central California coast to San Nicolas Island off southern California. The U.S. Fish and Wildlife Service began this translocation program in the summer of 1987. Any sea otters that wander away from San Nicolas Island into an "otter-free" management zone south of Point Conception must be captured if possible, and returned to their original central California residence to lessen the impact of otters on southern California recreational and commercial shellfisheries.

By July 1990, a total of 139 sea otters had been flown out to the island. The otters received first-class treatment during their plane trip to their new home. Large blocks of blue ice in their kennels kept them cool, while Fish and Wildlife "flight attendants" served them freshwater ice chips.

So far, only about 16 otters remain at San Nicolas Island, including some animals that were probably born here, despite the abundant food resources. For some reason, the population has remained stable since November 1989, although 40 pups have been born at the island and at least 12 of these are known to have survived to weaning age. The keen homing abilities of relocated otters surprised biologists, who found that 33 otters swam all the way back to their original mainland home, including some who were sighted back at their initial capture sites! Eleven otters are known or thought to have died. As many as 81 disappeared, and their fates are still a mystery. A few of the San Nicolas Island otters swam to the southern California mainland and a small group of otters was discovered on San Miguel Island, which was probably also from the translocated population. These "explorers" were either captured and moved out of the Management Zone or moved on their own.

A sea otter is carried to the shore at San Nicolas Island for release as part of the U.S. Fish and Wildlife translocation project.

Was the translocation a success? It doesn't look promising, but there's still a chance that the colony will begin to grow. Although results have been discouraging so far, they are similar to the initial patterns observed during previous successful translocations. Transplanted populations often decline when first moved to their new home, then gradually begin to increase after several years. Many people—fishermen, biologists and sea otter conservationists—anxiously await the final outcome in California.

Resource Benefits Sea otters and people don't always conflict. The presence of sea otters along the central California coast has beneficial environmental and economic impacts as well. Sea otters help the forests of giant kelp (*Macrocystis pyrifera*) flourish by eating the sea urchins that graze heavily on the kelp. And people commercially harvest giant kelp to extract a remarkable substance called algin, which is used to make over 500 products including ice cream, yogurt, beer, paint, toothpaste, shaving cream and even dissolvable surgical thread. The California kelp industry reaps a rich harvest of about $50 million worth of kelp each year.

California has a thriving tourism industry, and many people travel to coastal communities to watch sea otters, boosting local economies. The protected status of sea otters actually helps protect much of California's most attractive and pristine coastline from the development of offshore oil and gas resources because these activities endanger sea otters. Other threats to the California population include shooting, pollution and habitat degradation, as human activities such as jet skiing encroach on the sea otters' home. California sea otters are classified as "threatened" under the federal Endangered Species Act, "depleted" under the Marine Mammal Protection Act, and as a "fully protected mammal" under California state law.

A tagged sea otter heads for the ocean, while researchers track it using radio telemetry. While only 17 otters had made San Nicolas Island their home as of 1996, biologists remain hopeful, since transplanted populations often decline then slowly increase.

Monterey Bay Aquarium Otters

The Monterey Bay Aquarium offers intimate views of California sea otters—views you seldom get in nature. You'll often see the aquarium otters playing and frolicking like giant wet puppies. When not resting or feeding, they wrestle, somersault, shake, pounce, paw, lunge, chase, grab, bite, push and shove. In the wild it's usually the young otters, especially groups of juvenile males along the coast, that spend much of their time engaged in this rough play. It's no wonder that we find sea otters so endearing.

The sea otters living at the Monterey Bay Aquarium were once tiny orphaned pups rescued by local residents or wildlife biologists and brought to the aquarium. It's almost miraculous that these orphans survived, since sea otter pups are very delicate and difficult to care for. Before 1984, almost all orphaned California otter pups died within a few weeks of their rescue. Today, methods for raising otter pups have vastly improved, due to more knowledge about these sensitive

marine mammals and husbandry procedures developed by aquarium staff.

The first otter orphan to arrive at the aquarium was Jiggs, a four-week-old male who was found at Point Lobos State Reserve on February 16, 1984. He was quickly followed by Goldie, a five-week-old female rescued at Asilomar State Beach on February 22. Jiggs and Goldie soon formed a bond with each other and became inseparable. Both pups had to be carried everywhere together or they'd begin to cry. Soon, another orphaned female, christened Hailey, joined the aquarium's otter family. Weak and very sick, three-week-old Hailey washed ashore at Carmel Beach on March 28.

A third female orphan was Milkdud, who earned her name by repeatedly spilling her formula all over herself. Milkdud was one of twins born near San Simeon and abandoned by her mother, who couldn't raise both pups. Milkdud was only one day old and weighed a mere two-and-a-half pounds when rushed

The aquarium's sea otters captivate visitors of all ages. Hailey, above, was rescued from Carmel Beach as a weak, starving three-week-old pup in 1984. Now a full-grown and healthy adult, Hailey has formed a strong bond with another female otter named Goldie.

Goldie perches on rocks in the exhibit, giving visitors a close-up glimpse of how an otter moves on land.

to the aquarium on October 4, 1984. She was the youngest and smallest wild otter pup successfully raised in the aquarium's otter rescue and care program. The fact that Milkdud was a twin makes her even more special because female sea otters almost always bear only one pup at a time. Unfortunately, after nine years at the aquarium Milkdud died of complications from pneumonia.

A close bond formed between Milkdud and Hailey, who used to behave maternally toward Milkdud, grooming and protecting her like a pup, and even letting her steal food. Now Hailey and Goldie share a close bond with one another.

The youngest otter in the exhibit is now a curious and playful male named Roscoe who replaced Jiggs a few months after he died in August, 1986. Two-week-old Roscoe was found on March 26, 1986, on a beach near the Monterey Harbor.

2

Otters and Kin

Sea otters (*Enhydra lutris*) belong to one of the four major groups of former land mammals that have adapted to life in the sea. The other three marine mammal groups include the pinnipeds (seals, sea lions, fur seals and walruses); sirenians (manatees and dugongs); and cetaceans (whales, porpoises and dolphins). Polar bears aren't included in these four major divisions, even though they also have some adaptations to ocean life.

Although marine mammals differ from land mammals in many respects, both groups share fundamental features of mammals: being warm-blooded, using lungs to breathe air, having hair or fur, and nursing their young with mammary glands. The production of milk by females sets mammals apart from all other animals.

Scientists believe that sea otters descended from a primitive fish-eating otterlike ancestor about five to seven million years ago, during the late Miocene/early Pliocene period. Otters probably entered the ocean to avoid predators and to search for new sources of food. These ancestral otters, finding abundant food along the shore, remained there generation after generation, gradually adapting to living in the ocean.

Sea otters are the slowest-swimming and least streamlined group of marine mammals. Although their hindfeet have become webbed and flipperlike, otters have retained the front paws of a land carnivore. While sea otters are the most recently evolved group of marine mammals, they have no ties to land, unlike seals which must still return to land to breed and molt. Sea otters can breed, give birth and raise their young entirely at sea.

Sea otters belong to the mustelid family, which also includes freshwater otters, weasels, minks, skunks and badgers. Most mustelids

Among the largest members of their clan, male sea otters reach lengths of over four feet, while females average just under four feet.

The largest relatives of sea otters, giant Amazonian otters, below, may measure six to eight feet, nose to tail. These otters, above, have distinctive white fur on their chests.

have long, slender bodies, short legs, rounded ears and anal scent glands. All of the mustelids are carnivores, or "meat-eating" predators. Although sea otters are the second smallest of the marine mammals, they're one of the largest mustelids, measuring about four feet in length from tip of nose to tail and weighing up to 100 pounds. (Only the giant Amazonian otter, *Pteronura brasiliensis*, exceeds them in length.) The average adult California female sea otter weighs only about 44 pounds, while the average male weighs 64 pounds. Otters from certain areas of Alaska are somewhat larger. Like other species of otters, male sea otters probably live for 10 to 15 years, while the lifespan of females is estimated to be about 15 to 20 years.

The sea otter is one of nine to 13 species of otters found throughout the world (otter specialists don't agree on the exact number of species). Besides sea otters, only one other otter lives in the ocean—the rare marine otter (*Lutra felina*), sometimes called the "sea cat." Marine otters are the smallest species of otter, as well as marine mammal. At about nine pounds, they're not much bigger than a house cat. The few remaining sea cats in the world live in kelp beds off Chile and Peru in South America, where they occasionally swim up freshwater rivers in search of prawns. The dwindling population of marine otters is now classified as endangered.

North American river otters, top, are smaller than sea otters, and live in fresh water. The Asian small-clawed otter (Aonyx capensis), below, is one of the smallest in the otter clan at 6 to 12 pounds.

Like sea otters, marine otters were also heavily hunted for their fur by early whalers and settlers from Tierra del Fuega.

Besides sea otters and marine otters, all other otters live in fresh water, although some river otters (*Lutra canadensis*) travel freely between the ocean and rivers along the coast of the Pacific Northwest. How else do sea otters and river otters differ? Although the two species resemble one another in appearance, sea otters are larger, perhaps two or three times heavier than river otters. Their large bodies help sea otters conserve heat in cold ocean waters. The hindfeet of sea otters look like large flippers, and are webbed to the tips of their toes. Although the river otter's hindfeet are webbed, they're fairly small and not very flipperlike. The sea otter's tail is flattened and somewhat paddlelike, while the river otter's tail is longer and rounder in appearance, tapering to a point. The forepaws of sea otters have short claws that, while not retractile like those of a cat, can be extended. On the other hand, the foreclaws of the river otter cannot be extended or retracted.

Sea otters generally swim belly-up on their backs while paddling with their hindflippers. They're clumsy on land and spend most of their time in the water. River otters swim belly-down, with their backs nearly submerged. And they often remain on land where they move about easily and gracefully. River otters will travel several miles over land to reach another lake or stream, often playing "slip-and-slide" down slick, muddy or snowy slopes along the way. Sea otter juveniles and pups are also quite playful, although adults don't play as much as grown river otters.

North American river otters move about easily on land as well as on ice and snow.

Like other marine mammals, sea otters bear a single pup, while river otters may give birth to up to four young in a litter. Finally, river otters, adept at catching fishes, frogs, crayfish, snails, and certain rodents and birds, eat a more varied diet than sea otters, which feed on marine invertebrates and, in some parts of Alaska, catch fishes.

Subspecies of Sea Otters   Not all sea otters in the North Pacific are exactly alike. While to us, differences in the appearance and behavior of Russian sea otters compared to California sea otters may seem slight, scientists separate sea otters into three different subspecies, or races, based on differences in skull characteristics and genetic components.

Subspecies are genetically different populations of a species that live in separate geographical ranges. One sea otter subspecies, the Russian sea otter (*Enhydra lutris lutris*), lives in the Kuril Islands and along the eastern coast of the Kamchatka Peninsula north to the Commander Islands. The Alaskan sea otter (*Enhydra lutris kenyoni*) is found along Alaska's Aleutian Island chain to Prince William Sound and southward to Washington. The third subspecies is the California sea otter (*Enhydra lutris nereis*), which is found only along the coast of central California (and off San Nicolas Island), but was probably once common from northern California south to near Punta Abreojos in Baja California.

The California population is now geographically and genetically isolated from other sea otter populations. It's the only naturally occurring (i.e., not translocated) sea otter population found south of Alaska in the contiguous United States, and we must continue to diligently protect the small remaining population of sea otters along the California coast.

Alaskan sea otters, like this mother and pup, haul out on land more frequently in some areas than California sea otters.

Aquarium Otters and People

Behavioral conditioning, including the use of hand and voice signals, allows for safe interaction between aquarium staff and otters.

Years ago before the exhibit otters were trained, their independent and mischievous side emerged more often. They responded to newcomers in the water differently than their familiar caretakers, as a *National Geographic* underwater photographer discovered. One of the otters, perhaps thinking he had a giant rubber toy to romp with, bit a gaping hole in the diver's neoprene drysuit, chewed on expensive camera gear, and playfully ripped off the diver's face mask. That was the last time anyone but aquarium staff and volunteers swam in the exhibit with the otters.

Now the female otters remain in the exhibit and have grown accustomed to staff divers as they clean the rockwork and acrylic windows three times a week. During cleaning times, the big male Roscoe gets a short vacation in the holding pool.

The aquarium otters now participate in a daily training program, which provides these curious and intelligent animals with a more stimulating environment, and promotes cooperative and safe interactions between exhibit staff and otters. Training has helped the otters to adjust better to changes in their environment, such as behind-the-scenes film crews, and has made it much easier for staff to conduct husbandry and medical procedures. For instance, the otters open their mouths on request so staff can inspect their teeth, with no biting!

Trainers use hand and voice signals to direct otters. With positive reinforcement of correct behaviors, using food as a reward, the otters have learned to touch a buoy float attached to the end of a short pole, and to follow it as the trainer leads them to a desired location. The otters even search underwater for an object on request, and offer it to the trainers when asked. In the past, the staff had to trade a bribe of crab for any object in the otter's possession (usually a hard item for pounding on exhibit windows) or wait until the otter grew tired of its destructive plaything.

3

Sea Otters and Their Environment

If you look carefully into the kelp beds along the coast of central California, chances are you'll spot sea otters floating on the water's surface. Although from a distance a sea otter looks something like a little brown log, a closer look with binoculars reveals a whiskered, weasel-like face, stubby paws stiffly pointed skyward and large webbed hindflippers, all wrapped in a luxurious coat of rich brown fur.

Most sea otters along the California coast live very close to shore in waters with a rocky bottom and an abundance of kelp, although some otters are found along sandy shores. A few even travel into Elkhorn Slough at Moss Landing. An important part of good sea otter habitat is kelp, especially giant kelp. Otters forage and rest in kelp beds, often wrapping themselves securely in a "blanket" of kelp before taking a nap. Like us, sea otters are creatures of habit. Groups of otters, as well as individuals, prefer certain kelp beds as "local hang-outs." The abundance and distribution of the kelp canopy, which changes throughout the year, largely determines where you'll find large numbers of otters.

Otters on Land Do California sea otters ever come ashore? Yes, but it's hard to know just how frequently otters haul out because they blend into the rocks so well. Yet biologists know that California otters don't come ashore as often or in groups as large as Alaskan sea otters, which may rest onshore in groups of up to several hundred animals. California sea otters usually haul out on land alone or

California sea otters spend most of their life at sea near kelp forests, but occasionally haul out on intertidal rocks, as this female is doing, below left. She may be trying to rest or avoid an overzealous male.

in very small groups, although once 18 adults and four pups were spotted on shore along Pebble Beach. Otters usually prefer to haul out on low, easily accessible nearshore rocks cushioned with algae, but sometimes haul out on sand or cobble beaches. On land, sea otters move very awkwardly. (If we were walking around with a pair of swim fins on our feet, we'd move about rather clumsily, too.)

Aquarium researchers found that some individuals like to haul out on land more than others. One female, who had a long history of coming ashore, also dragged her pup onto the rocks with her. Her pup is now an adult female who hauls out in the same area as her mother. Another sea otter earned the nickname "Old MacDonald" when he crawled into a farmer's newly plowed field half a mile inland— a very un-otterlike thing to do. Researchers have also discovered that sexually receptive females tend to haul out very frequently, possibly because they're weak or are trying to avoid sexual advances from interested males. Yet an especially persistent male may come ashore in pursuit of a female, so the beach doesn't always provide a safe refuge. The time of year may also affect sea otters' hauling-out patterns—they seem to come ashore more frequently in late winter and spring when the kelp canopy is very sparse.

Otters and Kelp Forest Communities Sea otters can have a profound and complex effect on nearshore marine communities like kelp forests. Otters feed heavily on sea urchins and other invertebrates,

Kinky, an old male, came ashore more often than other otters. Many locals were fond of Kinky, who showed little fear of people.

which graze on giant kelp and other types of algae. By eating these animals and limiting their populations, sea otters allow kelp beds to flourish. As kelp forests expand, available shelter and nutrients increase, providing homes for a rich and diverse group of plants and animals. With the enhancement of the kelp forest, some fish populations also increase.

Of course, many other variables besides sea otters may affect the structure of nearshore kelp forest communities, including severe winter storms, changing climatic conditions such as the warm waters of El Niño in 1982–1983, water temperature, available nutrients, sunlight, and the many kinds of plant-grazing invertebrates. But extensive damage to kelp forests by sea urchins rarely occurs in areas where sea otters have lived for some time.

When sea otters are present, kelp forests tend to flourish. Otters feed heavily on sea urchins and other shellfish which graze on kelp and can devastate kelp forests when present in great numbers.

Skipper, above, bears a big scar on his lip from a white shark attack, which usually proves fatal to sea otters. White sharks, left, may kill more than 10 percent of the otters that are found dead.

Sea Otter Predators Besides humans, the only other predator of sea otters in California waters is the great white shark, *Carcharodon carcharias*. Even a minor white shark bite can kill a sea otter. Yet one fortunate otter named "Skipper" survived a white shark attack after a week of recuperation at the aquarium's "otter hospital." Skipper, retrieved from Moss Landing Harbor, had open cuts on his face and forelegs which were stitched by the aquarium's veterinarian Tom Williams.

After tagging and releasing Skipper at Moss Landing, aquarium researchers followed him. Slowly but steadily he appeared to recover, although a large adult male otter often stole his food, taking advantage of Skipper's weakened condition. Skipper currently resides with a group of males in Santa Cruz. You can tell him apart from the other otters by the permanently pouty expression on his healed lips, a trait that's earned him the nickname "Scarlip."

White sharks appear to kill about ten percent of the California sea otters that are found dead. Biologists often find shark tooth fragments embedded in the flesh of lacerated sea otters. Most of the shark-bitten otters are found in the northern portion of their range, especially from Pebble Beach to Año Nuevo. Large seal rookeries at Año Nuevo probably attract white sharks, which may not actively search out and prey on otters, but instead mistake them for their preferred meal of harbor seals, sea lions or elephant seals. Near Año Nuevo Island, sea otter mortality caused by white sharks has been as high as 20 percent.

In some areas of Alaska and Russia, sea otters are killed by land predators. Coyotes (*Canis latrans*) in Prince William Sound kill juvenile sea otters hauled out on land, where they're easy prey. At Amchitka Island, bald eagles (*Haliaeetus leucocephalus*) capture and eat young sea otter pups. The eagles usually take the pups as they float on the surface while their mothers are under water diving for food. Along the Kamchatka Peninsula, brown bears (*Ursus arctos*) prey on sea otters. The hungry bears, emerging from hibernation, capture many of the otters at the end of winter when they come ashore to rest, weakened by the constant winter storms.

Home at the Aquarium

The Monterey Bay Aquarium's three "juvenile delinquents," as the aquarium guides used to call the otters on exhibit, have grown into adults ranging in age from 10 to 12 years and weighing about 50 pounds (the females) to 60 pounds (the male). They provide lively entertainment for aquarium visitors, and unlike most wild California otters, they often haul out on the concrete deck. Huddled together while sleeping or grooming, they may resemble one gigantic fur ball. Sometimes it's hard to see where one otter begins and the other ends.

Years ago when the otters were first introduced to their new home at about eight months of age, their skillful little paws unscrewed and unbolted many parts of the exhibit. They picked up small loose rocks from the bottom and banged them against the sides of the exhibit so often that the plexiglass windows became cloudy with scratches. One otter actually succeeded in removing a 17-pound rock from the bottom and wrestling it onto the deck. Even a water jet and steel bolt on the bottom of the exhibit became the objects of otter curiosity.

After removing the implements of destruction, the aquarium caretakers provided their charges with small rubber and plastic toys. Mysteriously, the toys disappeared. Were the otters eating them? A diver finally discovered the stash of toys inside pipes supplying water to the exhibit. Apparently, the otters had been hiding their toys in the crevices for quite some time.

In the past when the exhibit was being cleaned, the otters used to spend the night in another tank, where they were given new "toys" like rocks and clams that would ordinarily scratch the exhibit windows. When returned to the exhibit the next morning, the otters always seemed very lethargic and tired. After some worry about the possible medical causes of these morning blues, caretakers discovered that the otters were wearing themselves out during all-night parties with their new toys.

Today otters have an even larger selection of entertaining yet "nonscratch" toys to play with, and they live in a new multi-species exhibit, which represents a more natural environment for the otters and includes various types of algae, fish and invertebrates. When first introduced to the new exhibit occupants, the otters turned the sea stars (*Asterina miniata*) into snack food, and carried the gumboot chitons (*Cryptochiton stelleri*) about like toys. Needless to say, these animals did not thrive and are no longer exhibit residents. Large *Macrocystis* kelp plants do not last in the exhibit either, since the otters have a special fondness for this particular kelp and continuously tug, pull and chew at these plants, which must be replenished often in the exhibit.

Our playful exhibit sea otters make everything a game. A basketball makes a perfect toy that can't be hidden under water and won't scratch exhibit windows. Even water hoses become playthings for these rambunctious otters, who've accidently squirted people by pressing the nozzle.

4

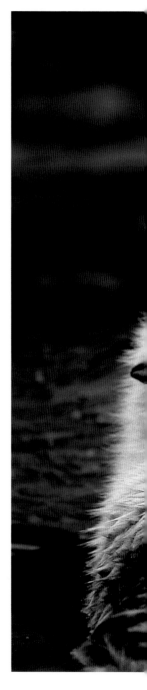

Survival in the Sea

Imagine how uncomfortable you'd feel as a thin-skinned, air-breathing mammal living in the ocean—trying to keep warm, find food and care for your young. Sea water presents a special set of challenges for air-breathing, warm-blooded mammals like seals and sea otters. Yet like other marine mammals, sea otters have evolved a number of remarkable adaptations for coping with life in the sea.

The World's Warmest Fur Cold ocean water rapidly draws heat out of the body. Sea otters live in waters ranging from 35° to 60°F, yet they must maintain a constant body temperature of close to 100°F, a process known as thermoregulation. Unlike whales and other marine mammals, sea otters have very little blubber to protect them from the cold. Instead, otters depend on their remarkably dense, water-resistant fur to insulate them against the chilly waters.

A sea otter's velvety fur is made up of two layers. The long outer guard hairs give the otter its overall soft and fuzzy appearance. As the name implies, these guard hairs form a protective covering that helps keep the underfur dry, since the outer hairs lie extremely flat when the animal is immersed in water. Underneath the guard hair layer is the extremely fine and dense underfur. Depending on which part of the body you examine, one square inch of sea otter underfur contains between 170,000 to over 1,000,000 hairs, more than that of any other animal on earth. By comparison, a dog has about 1,000 to 60,000 hairs per square inch, and people have an average of about 100,000 hairs on their heads.

The color of sea otter fur is usually dark brown, but some otters have grizzled, or very light-colored, fur on their head, neck, chest or forelegs. This grizzling effect is due to the gradual loss of brown pigment in the guard hair, the same way our hair becomes streaked with gray as it loses pigmentation. The heads of some otters may appear nearly white. The fur of many otter lightens with age, although you may see dark-headed older adults as well as light-headed youngsters.

Keeping Warm and Clean Sea otters must spend much of their time grooming and cleaning their fur to maintain its special insulating qualities. When you see an otter energetically somersaulting and rubbing its body, it's not only cleaning the fur but also trapping air bubbles within the millions of tiny fur fibers. This layer of entrapped air provides buoyancy and an insulating bubble barrier that keeps the skin dry under water. If you could run your hand through a

Sea otters depend on their thick, velvety fur for survival in the cold ocean. The dark brown fur of older adults sometimes becomes grizzled or nearly white.

Female #513, left, grooms herself in Monterey Harbor. Grooming involves a sequence of four stages, beginning with energetic somersaulting and rolling and ending with the otter slowly licking its paws, chest and face. This otter, below left, is in stage three—licking and rubbing its hind-flippers and tail.

submerged sea otter's fur, the soft, air-bubble packed underfur would actually seem to feel dry! Grooming also increases skin circulation, and spreads natural oils on the skin and fur. The otter has special glands that secrete oil, enhancing the water-repellent quality of the fur.

While grooming, an otter is amazingly dexterous—twisting, bending and somersaulting as if it lived inside a suit of skin several sizes too large. The sea otter's loosely articulated skeleton and lack of a collarbone promote this flexibility, allowing it to groom every part of its fur. When does an otter groom? Watch for energetic grooming bouts after an otter eats and upon waking up.

It's this life-saving fur that makes sea otters, of all the marine mammals, the most vulnerable to the effects of oil contamination. If an otter's fur becomes soiled with oil or other pollutants, the protective bubble barrier is destroyed and the fur becomes matted, losing its insulating properties. Cold ocean water will reach the skin and begin to draw heat away from the animal. Without protection from the cold, the otter can no longer regulate its body temperature. This usually leads to life-threatening hypothermia, or extreme chilling, and other complications that result in the otter's death from exposure, as well as from ingesting the toxic oil as it tries to groom.

Burning Calories Sea otters also keep warm by burning calories at a rapid rate, something many people wish they could do. The metabolic rate of sea otters is about two to three times higher than that of a similar-sized land mammal. In order to maintain this elevated metabolic rate, a sea otter must frequently eat large amounts of food. A wild adult sea otter eats the equivalent of about 23 to 33 percent of its total body weight each day. A 50-pound wild otter would have to eat about 11 to 16 pounds of food (or 4,300 to 5,750 calories) every 24 hours just to stay alive. For a 150-pound person, this would amount to eating 35 to 40 pounds of food each day!

The sea otter at left is rocking itself through the water and sculling with its tail while keeping its paws and flippers warm and dry. Some, like the otter above, rest with their paws over their eyes,

Conserving Heat Have you ever wondered why sea otters rest on the surface with their forepaws rigidly extended above the water? Keeping their forelimbs dry while resting is another way otters conserve heat. Otters also often lie still with their hindflippers folded over their abdomens to keep them dry. An otter's paws, as well as the thinly webbed hindflippers, have little or no fur as well as a large surface area where body warmth can be quickly lost to the colder water. When a resting sea otter stretches or is disturbed, it's often so reluctant to wet its dry paws and hindflippers that it will continue to hold forepaws and sometimes hindflippers high in the air while carefully swimming or completely rolling in its remarkably loose skin. A dry otter may undulate its torso and "rock" or slowly "inch-worm" its way to another spot to avoid getting wet.

Aquarium researchers have even found that certain individuals have favorite resting positions. Some otters rest with both paws covering their eyes, as if to shield them from the sun. Others sleep with both forelimbs splayed in a "V" at an angle, or with only one paw raised up in the air, or with both paws pushed together.

Moving through the Water Sea otters usually swim belly-up on the surface, alternately pumping their hindflippers up and down, somewhat like pedaling a bicycle. When an otter needs to travel quickly, it swims on its stomach and undulates its entire body. Adult males often swim like this when patrolling the boundaries of their territories or in pursuit of sexually receptive females. Compared to highly streamlined whales and seals, sea otters swim slowly at speeds of about two to three miles per hour—the speed of an average human swimmer. Otters don't need to move fast because they feed mainly on stationary or very sluggish prey. Still, sea otters have distinctive adaptations that allow them to move through the water with less resistance. Their broadly flattened tails enhance propulsion.

In addition, the hindflippers are webbed and the toes are progressively lengthened so that the fifth or outer digit is the longest—just the opposite pattern of our toes. This type of hindflipper helps an otter swim more efficiently on its back while at the surface.

Diving in the Ocean   While diving for food, sea otters must conserve oxygen and contend with underwater pressure. They generally forage in shallow waters of less than 60 feet, and their feeding dives usually last one to two minutes. Yet sea otters have been known to dive to depths of 330 feet and remain under water for up to four or five minutes. In contrast, a person without oxygen passes out within three minutes. Sea otters can hold their breath for such a long time in part because their lungs are nearly two-and-a-half times larger than the lungs of a similar-sized mammal. Large lungs help store oxygen and regulate buoyancy while the otter floats on the surface. And sea otters have flexible ribs that allow the lungs to collapse under pressure. Otters also have cartilaginous airways connected directly to tiny, air-filled lung sacs, or alveoli, which help provide an unrestricted flow of oxygen to the blood. In addition, the sea otter's blood has a higher buffering capacity than that of nondiving mammals, which helps the otter handle the excess carbon dioxide that accumulates under pressure during a dive.

Sea otters have large hindflippers that propel them while they swim on their backs at the surface. Otters that are in a hurry or males patrolling their territories often swim on their stomachs.

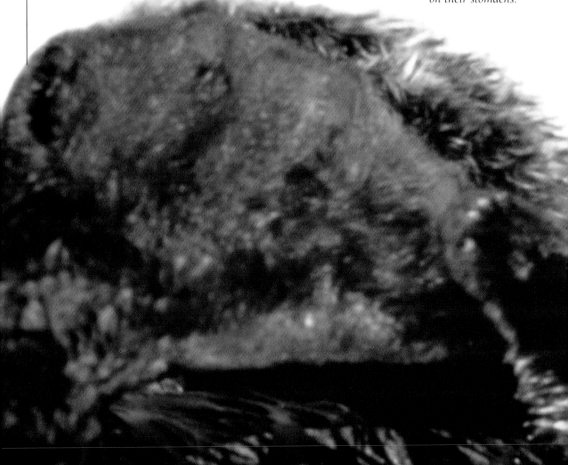

Sea otters spend about one-third of each 24-hour period diving for food and eating it at the surface. Otters typically dive to depths of 30 to 40 feet for about a minute or so.

The Senses   We still know very little about how sea otters see, hear and smell both in the water and on land. Yet biologists know that their eyesight, hearing and sense of smell have been modified from those of land carnivores to help otters forage and communicate in the ocean.

Sea otters can see clearly both in air and under water. If you've tried to look around beneath the surface without a face mask, you know how blurry vision becomes under water. When you, or other land mammals, submerge in water, your eyes are no longer able to bend light rays sufficiently to see clearly, because the cornea (the transparent convex structure covering your eye) cannot focus images under water. It turns out that the cornea and water have the same refractive index, resulting in farsightedness. A face mask lets you see clearly under water by forming an air barrier that allows your eyes to focus as on land.

To cope with this problem of farsightedness, sea otters have an exceptionally well-developed accommodative ability of the eyeball which changes the refractive power of the lens as necessary. This compensates for the refractive loss of the cornea under water and allows the otter to focus on objects both in water and in air. The sea otter's eye, like a seal's eye, also seems to be protected from the elements by a tough outer covering, called a corneal epithelium.

Sea otters, like seals and most nocturnal carnivores that need to see well at night or in dark, murky waters, appear to have a well-developed tapetum. The *tapetum lucidum* is a specialized layer in back of the retina that contains many guanine crystals. These crystals allow the retina to reflect light like a mirror and give it a shiny metallic appearance. This helps the eye gather light in dimly lit environments. The tapetum causes a cat's eyes to glow in the dark, as would a sea otter's eyes if you were to shine a flashlight at them during the night.

A sea otter's long, sensitive whiskers, combined with its forepaws, help it find and capture prey under water.

Sea otters appear to have a good sense of touch. Long and sensitive whiskers help them detect vibrations in the water and find prey in murky depths. Otters' sensitive forepaws also help them locate and capture prey under water. Divers report watching otters search for food by patting rocks and feeling into crevices with their paws, sometimes while looking elsewhere. The aquarium's exhibit otters feel around the bottom of their exhibit in a similar manner.

Scientists don't really know how well sea otters hear. Like North American river otters, they seem most sensitive to high frequencies. A sea otter's ears are small and somewhat curled. Held erect while at the surface, their ears fold sharply downward during dives.

Otters seem to have an excellent sense of smell and taste. Inside an otter's nose, an extensive honeycomb of bones suggests that otters have an acute sense of smell. An experienced otter watcher will often observe otters sniffing the air and the water's surface, as well as other otters. When one otter approaches another, it usually noses, nuzzles or nibbles the other's head, abdomen and especially the hindflipper area. Adult male otters probably locate and identify sexually receptive females by scent cues. Males can detect receptive females from quite a distance—as much as a mile or more away.

In a blur of action, a sea otter "periscopes" high out of the water before diving to look more closely at something.

Living in Salt Water If you think you have problems dealing with excess sodium in your diet, imagine the water balance problems facing sea otters and other marine mammals that spend their entire lives in sea water. Otters and most other marine mammals are constantly in danger of losing water to the more concentrated, or salty, ocean in which they live. They must keep the osmotic concentration of their body fluids constant despite their saltwater environment, a process known as osmoregulation. And besides living in sea water, California sea otters eat marine invertebrates that have an elevated salt content, much higher than that of fishes, and often as high as that of the surrounding sea water. This salty diet raises the otter's "salt load" even further.

Sea otters conserve water and maintain a suitable water balance by means of their large, heavily lobulated kidneys. Their kidneys are very efficient at concentrating urine by absorbing water and eliminating excess salt in urea, a waste product that's more concentrated than ocean water. Wild otters also drink sea water, which may help them process and eliminate urea. Curiously enough, exhibit otters living at the aquarium sometimes drink fresh water from a hose and sprinklers that clean the windows.

5

Sea Otter Diets

If you see an otter in the waters off Pacific Grove near Otter Point whacking snails on a rock, chances are good that you're watching territorial male #534, nicknamed "Nosebuster" because of the rough way he treats a female's nose while mating. Nosebuster loves to eat turban snails (*Tegula* spp.). He'll ignore most other prey.

Female #220, who was affectionately known to researchers as "Suckerface" because of her fondness for octopus, ate turban snails too, but also liked octopus (*Octopus* sp.) and purple sea urchins (*Strongylcentrotus purpuratus*). Both Suckerface and female #508 were remarkably successful in capturing the cryptic octopus. In one feeding bout off the aquarium, female #508 ate over 20 small octopus. Female #182, an older adult female who lived along Cannery Row and Pacific Grove, specialized in mussels (*Mytilus* sp.) and abalone (*Haliotis* spp.). Female #520 especially liked fat innkeeper worms (*Urechis caupo*). Another female, known as "Flathead," favored sea urchins, crabs and sea stars (*Pisaster* spp.). Like other otters, Flathead often ate only the tips of the sea star's arms, sucked out the gonads, then tossed it back in the ocean where it's "recycled" since the star usually regenerates new arms.

One of the more fascinating findings to emerge from research on tagged Monterey Bay sea otters is that, like many people, otters have favorite foods, at least in areas where they've lived for some time. From over 33 available types of marine invertebrates on the menu, an otter tends to specialize in only one, two or three types of prey. Aquarium researchers tried to discover how an otter acquires its preference for certain foods. Do pups learn what to eat by observing their mothers?

Researchers found that three adult females have eaten the same foods as their mothers since they were weaned, and several dependent pups did so while still with their mothers. One mother and her daughter ate mainly kelp crabs (*Pugettia* spp.) and sea urchins. Another mother, female #190, and her offspring ate a lot of rock oysters (*Pododesmus cepio*). Female #190's daughter, known to researchers as "Tubehead," also used a glass bottle to dislodge rock oysters and other shellfish under water, just like her mother.

Another daughter, #535, employed a truly one-of-a-kind foraging tactic researchers call "surfgrass salad bar," a technique her mother used when #535 was a pup. Like her mother, #535 dove to the bottom and retrieved a large clump of surf grass—often attached to a rock—placed it on her chest at the surface and leisurely picked out tiny kelp crabs and other small munchables.

Although the otter at left is eating a sea urchin, each sea otter has its favorite food, and some don't eat urchins at all. Otters that specialize in prey such as abalone, like the otter below, can be remarkably successful at finding them even when this prey becomes scarce in areas where otters have lived for some time.

Abalone
Haliotis *sp.*

Rock crab
Cancer antennarius

Brown turban snail
Tegula brunnea

The intriguing finding that mothers pass their unique food-gathering strategies on to their pups could mean that competition for food is reduced in areas that otters have lived in for some time, since each otter searches for different prey. If daughters have pups of their own and pass along their own menu preferences, these individual foraging patterns might persist in a given area for generations.

On the other hand, otters recolonizing new areas in general prefer abalone, rock crab (*Cancer* spp.) and large red sea urchins (*Strongylocentrotus franciscanus*)—all foods packed full of rich calories. After otters live in an area for some time and their favorite foods become scarce, they will also eat other prey, including purple sea urchins, kelp crabs, clams, turban snails, mussels, rock scallops (*Hinnites giganteus*), rock oysters, octopuses, barnacles (*Balanus* spp.), sea stars, fat innkeeper worms and chitons. Although many Alaskan otters feed on bottom fishes, California otters rarely do so. At Amchitka Island and in other areas of Alaska where otters have lived for a long time, fishes make up an important part of the diet, probably because of their abundance compared to the more scarce urchins and other invertebrates.

Sea otters in Monterey Bay also take advantage of seasonally abundant foods, like pelagic red crabs and squid. Otters feasting on a seemingly endless supply of spawning squid create quite a spectacle. While gorging themselves, squid tentacles dangle from the otters' mouths and their unique storage spots in their armpits as they continuously try to steal the slippery prey from each other.

Where Otters Eat California otters usually forage for food close to shore among kelp plants or along the rocky bottom in water less

Each otter specializes in only one to three kinds of prey, which might include one of the choice marine invertebrates shown above.

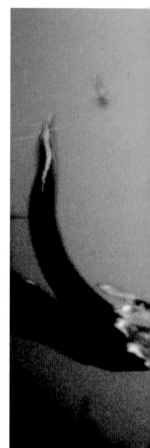

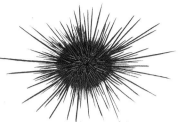

Purple sea urchin
Strongylocentrotus purpuratus

Red octopus
Octopus rubescens

Red sea urchin
Strongylocentrotus franciscanus

than 60 feet. Yet they're capable of diving to more than five times this depth. Some of the territorial males in Monterey Bay dive offshore to depths of 100 to 130 feet. Juvenile males in the center of the range tend to feed farther offshore in deeper water than other otters. These young males may forage over one mile from shore—too far to see even with powerful telescopes.

In areas with sandy or muddy bottoms, otters dive to search for clams, rapidly digging up the bottom with their forelegs, much like a dog digging in the dirt. Large craters often mark the bottom where otters have scooped out the sand. Sometimes an otter won't even bother to dive for a meal. It may forage along the shoreline in inter-tidal areas and dine on mussels. Or an otter may pluck kelp crabs or shake turban snails from the thick kelp canopy at the surface.

The otter above has just captured a large red sea urchin. Other items on sea otter menus include Pisaster sea stars, far left, and rock crabs, near left.

Stealing a Meal   Resourceful otters may simply steal another otter's food at the surface, instead of working to get their own prey. Aside from dependent pups that constantly snatch food from their mothers, adult territorial males are the most common thieves, taking prey from females and mother-pup pairs.

Females only occasionally pilfer food, and always steal from other females. Both male and female food-stealers tend to take the same type of prey that they capture on their own. Although males seem to gain substantial benefits from stealing food, the overall impact to female victims is quite low, probably because many female otters occupy one male's territory, and females range throughout an area encompassing the territories of several males.

Once when he was pair-bonded with a female, Nosebuster constantly solicited and stole prey from his mate as if he were her pup! And she tolerated this "immature" behavior, even offering her food to him at times. Surprisingly, most females don't protest or resist when males steal their food.

Territorial males occasionally employ an interesting and clever strategy called "hostage behavior" in which the male approaches and grabs a pup while its mother forages under water. The pup is relinquished to its mother only when she gives the male her prey in apparent "exchange" for her offspring.

Otters not only have to fend off other otters who try to steal their prey, but occasionally are harassed by gulls looking for food.

Otters have sharp teeth for holding slippery food like squid, while flattened molars help crush hard-shelled prey.

Otters, like the one feeding on abalone at left, usually dislodge the shellfish under water by smashing it with a rock, leaving a telltale hole in the middle of the shell

How Otters Eat Under water, an otter uses extremely powerful forelegs and paws to pry loose abalone and rock scallops. Unlike the hindclaws, the surprisingly sharp foreclaws can be extended when the otter flexes its paws. When captured, the harmless-looking sea otter can put up quite a struggle with its strong forelegs and powerful jaws. If you were to arm-wrestle with a sea otter, the otter would probably win.

A sea otter often stores the food it gathers under water in loose pouches of skin located under each foreleg. On the surface, an otter mysteriously producing one piece of food after another is actually just reaching into its full pouches. Otters can stuff these pouches with several prickly purple urchins at one time.

Otters will take advantage of seasonally available food, like this pelagic red crab, left, abundant during "El Niño" years.

The female at left, enjoying a meal of rich abalone meat, has a very distinctive nose scar acquired when she mated.

Holding wriggling prey like crabs at the surface takes a bit more skill. Otters often use their hindflippers to imprison crabs on their lower bellies while busily eating other morsels. Sea otters also rely on a behavior that aquarium researchers called "kelp bondage," or "straitjacketing." The otter wraps the crab tightly in kelp fronds draped over its belly to immobilize it while eating another prey item.

Unlike most carnivores, sea otters have broad, flattened molars ideal for crushing the hard-shelled foods they eat. Imagine chewing open a clam shell with your teeth, or nibbling on sharp sea urchin spines. Many otters eat so many purple sea urchins that their teeth, skulls and skeletons become stained purple. Old otters often develop extremely worn teeth, as might be expected from such constant wear and tear.

Using the rock on its stomach as a tool, the otter pounds a clam against it to break open the shell. Recent research shows that individual otters differ in their choice of tools and how they use them.

Tool Use Sea otters, along with only a few other animals, are unique in their use of tools. Other tool-using animals include some birds, chimpanzees, dolphins and, of course, people.

Otters often use rocks under water to pry loose or bash stubborn abalones or sea urchins wedged in crevices. And while floating stomach-up on the surface, otters place rocks on their chest and pound snails, crabs or other prey against these tools to break open the tough outer shells. Another rock may also serve as a hammer. Rocks aren't the only likely otter tool. They'll make good use out of old shells, driftwood, crab carapaces and even empty glass bottles.

Aquarium researchers found that otters also show individual differences in the tools they choose to use. Female #182 almost always used a huge slab of concrete or a large flat rock placed on her belly like a table as she ate. She also carried this hefty tool under water to pry abalone from rocks. Female #190 made a habit of using a glass cola bottle under water to break off rock oysters attached to rocks in Monterey Harbor.

Otters feeding together on the same prey may capture and eat it differently. For instance, female #216 hammered her snails against a rock with light, quick "tap-taps," while her neighbor Nosebuster whacked his snails slowly and with great force. Female #184 grabbed clumps of mussels above the surface and opened them with a rock, while female #203, feeding only a few feet away, dove to get her mussels and actually ripped them apart with her teeth.

Pups learning to feed have been known to pound prey against a styrofoam cup, plastic bag or even mom's belly—not very effective tools. A pup may also pretend it has a rock resting on its belly and wave the food in the air with repeated pounding motions. Pups may even go through the motions without holding anything. Slick prey, like a turban snail, may slip out of the pup's paws and fly backward through the air. Fortunately, the pup can always depend on mom for a ready supply of food.

Female #557 picked up her mother's highly unusual habit of using a glass bottle, like the one resting on the otter's stomach in the foreground, to dislodge shellfish under water.

Always Learning Sea otters readily explore new ways to find food, leading biologists to conclude that they learn quickly and solve problems well. Versatile foraging behavior is important to an animal like the sea otter that must find and eat such large amounts of food each day just to survive.

Some otters will actually look for hand-outs from local boaters or divers—a risky habit. One otter learned to reach into a bucket of squid on the stern of a boat in Monterey Harbor. Another harbor otter, Josephine, often begged for bait fish from tourists and fishermen, and even stole such fish from large male California sea lions near the wharf.

A few sea otters in the Monterey Bay area, mainly adult males, have learned to capture and eat large seabirds such as Western grebes (*Aechmophorus occidentalis*), cormorants (*Phalacrocora* spp.), gulls (*Larus* spp.), common loons (*Gavia immer*) and surf scoters (*Melanitta perspicillata*). The otters capture the birds by grabbing them from under water while the bird rests on the surface— an action that takes planning and intelligence, especially for an animal accustomed to selecting stationary or slow-moving prey on the bottom. Biologists suspect only a few otters are responsible for most of the bird predation. One male at Point Lobos State Reserve appeared to prefer to eat Western grebes and surf scoters. Researchers have watched at least six grebes and scoters fall victim to surprise attacks by this bird-eater. And because many of the attacks on seabirds are clustered in specific areas, researchers speculate that some otters learn new foraging strategies by watching other otters.

*Western grebe
Aechmophorus
occidentalis*

One curious young male otter learned that small octopus hide in the discarded aluminum cans littering the floor of Monterey Harbor. The octopus oozes through the tiny opening to find shelter within the can. After picking up a suspiciously heavy can, the enterprising male otter would bite it open and extract the resident octopus. An octopus attempting to flee would have its tentacles bitten off to prevent escape. Biologists watched this young otter capture several octopus this way, and speculate that he probably ate many more in this novel fashion.

Mealtime

The aquarium's otters are fed a menu of rockcod, smelt, squid, clam meat and shrimp four times a day, and receive rock crab treats three times a week.

What do the aquarium's resident otters eat? Four times each day, they're fed rockcod, smelt, squid, clam meat, and shrimp. The otters eat an amount of food equal to 12 to 15 percent of their body weight daily; their food requirements seem to be less than that of wild otters.

Three times a week, the otters are treated to rock crabs. Because crab shells make superb toys for banging against and scratching the exhibit windows, the claws and carapaces are removed before crabs are offered in the exhibit. Roscoe, however, sometimes gets the hard claws when he's in the holding pool. In the past, whole crabs were served in a holding pool behind the exhibit. But the clever otters nipped off the hard black tips of the crab claws and saved them in their underarm pouches to play with later. The black crab claws were removed to prevent the otters from banging them on the exhibit windows. Even so, mischievous Hailey used to pass pieces of crab shell to Milkdud through the small holes connecting the holding pool to the exhibit pool, replenishing the supply of forbidden shells for window-banging. In the redesigned exhibit there can be no passing of shell pieces between the pool and exhibit, which are now separated by a solid door.

One of the otters' favorite "foods" is *Macrocystis* kelp. It's hard to know if they enjoy munching on this rubbery plant because of its novelty, its taste, or perhaps both. They seem to relish the stipes and bulbous gas floats, which they hold and eat like carrots as the kelp makes loud, satisfying popping sounds. While wild otters occasionally nibble on kelp, they don't seem to find it the delectable or fun-to-eat treat favored by the aquarium's otters.

In many ways, the aquarium's resident sea otters have an easier life than the free-ranging otters off the California coast. To people who watch sea otters snoozing contentedly in the kelp, a wild otter's life may seem enviable, but it's really not very easy at all. Wild otters must constantly forage for food, compete for mates and contend with heavy storms and rough seas. Roscoe, the aquarium's young male, has two females all to himself with no competition from a rival male. And the exhibit otters will not drown in fishing nets, be attacked by white sharks, get shot by people or die in an oil spill. So although they are not free, the exhibit otters seem quite content in their aquarium habitat—the only home they've ever known since they were orphaned.

6

Social Behavior

The social life of sea otters is in many ways still an intriguing mystery to biologists. There's much we don't fully understand about how otters interact and communicate, or how they relate as family or kin groups. Yet long-term observations of tagged individuals are gradually revealing more about otters' social organization and behavior. We know now, for example, that each otter has its own distinctive "personality."

Female #188 liked to rest alone away from other otters, dined on crabs and sea urchins, and never came ashore. Josephine, a young female followed by aquarium researchers since she was born, often hauled out on land and preferred to eat rock oysters and mussels. She often engaged in some very un-otterlike behaviors, such as bullying harbor seals at their haul-out sites, or stealing bait fish from sea lions, as described earlier. Josephine also climbed into kayaks—definitely taking the occupants by surprise, and ignoring the signs that warn people not to approach otters too closely.

An older male, christened Kinky, liked to eat clams and was remarkably relaxed around people. Kinky didn't hold a territory, but instead used Moss Landing Harbor as home base. He has often made a 20-mile trip between Moss Landing and the aquarium's Great Tide Pool, where he'd haul out, groom himself and eat many of the tide pool's resident invertebrates. Kinky even managed to get himself marooned in a slough adjacent to Moss Landing Harbor, where he fed on clams for several days before biologists decided he was truly "stuck," and moved him back to the harbor.

Although otters tend to forage alone, they gather in groups to rest and socialize.

Kinky, above, marooned himself in the slough at Moss Landing where he fed on clams and allowed photographers to approach closely.

Otters sometimes haul out among the harbor seals, left. Most of the time, seals and otters ignore each other, but one young female otter, "Josephine," perhaps unaware of proper "otter–seal etiquette," fearlessly pushes harbor seals out of her way when she wants to rest on their rock.

A Typical Day What's a typical day like for a sea otter? Actually, there aren't any "typical" otters, since individuals vary widely in their activity patterns. However, the majority of otters tend to feed early in the morning, again in the late afternoon and once more late at night or early in the morning. Each feeding bout lasts about two to three hours. Otters usually groom themselves before and after each feeding, and rest throughout the middle of the day. In general, California sea otters spend roughly half of each 24-hour period resting, over one-third feeding, and the rest of their day grooming, swimming and interacting with other otters. Juvenile females seem to spend more time feeding than other otters. Sea otters are equally active both night and day.

Home Ranges Do otters travel much? Researchers track their movements by tagging their hindflippers or implanting radio transmitters in individual otters. Each otter has its own radio frequency. The color of the tag on the otter's right hindflipper generally tells you about that particular otter's origins. Otters tagged in the Monterey area, for example, have a red, orange, pink or dark green right tag. Otters from Santa Cruz sport a light blue right tag, and those from Morro Bay are tagged with silver. The color and position of the left hindflipper tag is unique for each otter, and lets researchers tell it apart from all others.

By observing tagged individuals, researchers have learned that each year many males seasonally travel long distances of 40 to 60 miles or more to male groups at either end of the range. However, both territorial and nonterritorial males may make long-distance trips at any time of the year. How far a male travels varies a great deal from individual to individual, and depends in part on how far he

To capture and tag individual otters, California Fish and Game divers sneak up on otters from below. Scooters propel divers, who scoop the otter into the trap at the surface and secure the netting. Two balloons provide buoyancy.

lives from the male groups. Yet on any particular day, a male tends to remain in the same area, perhaps traveling along the coastline only a mile or so. Territorial males in Monterey Bay, for example, usually stay within the bounds of their small, half-mile territories.

Sea otters appear to have remarkably strong homing tendencies. Biologists reported that many of the otters translocated to San Nicolas Island swam back across large expanses of open ocean to reach the mainland sites where they were originally captured.

Researchers captured and moved a number of male sea otters from Shell Beach to Moss Landing, a distance of 180 miles, to see what they would do. Despite being moved such a long distance from their home, most of the otters seemed to know exactly where they were and how to get back to Shell Beach.

Many of the southern males held for two days at Moss Landing remained in the Monterey Bay area and did not swim back, at least not for a while. Some of the otters that were released immediately swam back to Shell Beach, while others first traveled 17 miles north to a male group near Soquel before heading home. One adult male released at Moss Landing moved north to Soquel Point, traveled home to Shell Beach, returned to Soquel Point again, and then swam south once more to Cayucos, 155 miles south of Soquel Point. He was last seen back at Soquel Point again!

How did this southern male, or any of the other males, know about the Soquel male group, and how did they navigate to find their way home and back to Soquel again? Some day, biologists hope to have the answers to these questions. Perhaps the entire California range is "home" to many male otters.

Females are sedentary by comparison. They generally remain for years within a 6- to 12-mile area, while some Monterey females

Tiny ear tags, barely visible on the otter below, help researchers identify individuals that have lost their hind-flipper tags.

Flipper tags identify the Abalone Farm male #210, bottom, who kidnapped females from other males' territories and dragged them back to his own turf.

live in an even smaller area of two to three miles for many years. Yet a number of females break this general rule and take long trips. One young female tagged just north of Morro Bay traveled almost 100 miles to the Monterey peninsula and settled along Cannery Row. An adult female moved from Monterey to San Simeon and back again, a round trip of about 175 miles. Over the past four years, three other tagged females routinely moved back and forth across Monterey Bay between Santa Cruz and Monterey. These "commuters" often seemed to return to Monterey to give birth to new pups.

Researchers followed female #532 for several years and learned that she preferred red abalone and rock crabs, and was always extremely attentive to her pups, earning her the nickname, "Supermom."

Otter "Rafts"   Although sea otters feed, mate and give birth away from other otters, they usually rest together in groups called "rafts." In California, rafts tend to be small, containing two to 12 animals, although larger rafts may include 40 to 50 otters. In contrast, resting groups of up to 2,000 otters have been seen in some parts of Alaska! Females and pups in both California and Alaska sometimes form "nursery groups" of mother-pup pairs. The juvenile males in California don't remain with these groups, and are often found much farther offshore than other otters, perhaps because they're excluded from the protected inshore areas by territorial males.

Most otters spend their lives in the company of their own sex, except for territorial males who have the privilege of resting in female groups. The different areas where females and males occur are often called, appropriately, female areas and male areas.

The center of the sea otter range between Monterey and Morro Bay is essentially one enormous female area. Here you'll find females of all ages, dependent pups, territorial adult males and some recently weaned juvenile males. Most of the otters you see from the Monterey Bay Aquarium decks are females and pups. In the mid-1970s, a

Sea otters usually rest in small groups called "rafts." With the exception of territorial males, females and males rest in separate groups.

large male group of up to 140 otters inhabited the kelp beds off the old Hovden Cannery where the aquarium now stands, before the males moved north to Santa Cruz.

Male areas generally occur at the northern and southern ends of the range—Año Nuevo to the north and the Pismo Beach area to the south—where the population is slowly expanding. Male groups are often found off sandy beaches at the range fronts, such as Moss Landing and Elkhorn Slough, Estero Bay and areas south of Morro Bay. Male otters also congregate in certain kelp beds near Soquel Point and Point Joe to the north, and Cayucos Point and Shell Beach to the south, and observations suggest that males may inhabit offshore areas in the central part of the range. These "bachelor" groups consist of juvenile, subadult and adult males.

Group sizes vary seasonally, building up in the winter and spring when more adult males move into the male areas. At this time of year, fewer opportunities exist for them to mate with sexually receptive females. Females and mother-pup pairs sometimes venture into these male areas, and a number of females now live in the Santa Cruz area.

In any group of resting otters, you'll see a variety of resting styles, some with paws over eyes, or held straight in the air, for instance.

If you carefully observe a group of otters, you'll see obvious as well as more subtle interactions between individuals. Large pups and especially juveniles spend much of their time socializing and playing. Young males in some bachelor groups engage in endless bouts of wildly energetic and lively play. Leaping high out of the water and latching onto one another's fur with their mouths and paws, this tangled mass of squirming otters looks very much like a litter of puppies at play. Young males in these groups may also engage in mock fights and practice mating.

Otter Communication We're only just beginning to learn how sea otters communicate with each other. One common form of communication is the "head jerk." A sea otter entering a raft of otters will typically make contact with the resting otters by nosing and sniffing their heads, chests, bellies or hindflipper areas while rapidly jerking its head from side-to-side, as though saying "no." Prolonged head jerking by a male may mean that he's located a sexually receptive female in estrus.

The recipient of the head jerk usually remains calm and ignores the other otter. But occasionally, the disturbed otter will lunge or snap at the intruder, or employ a "tail block" by holding the tail over its belly between the hindflippers, effectively blocking the hindflipper area. Sometimes a particularly exuberant otter will wake an entire group of dry, peacefully sleeping otters by splashing and pouncing on each of them in turn. Researchers trying to identify resting otters appreciate these "rude" and disruptive intruders because the disturbed otters will often roll over and show their hindflipper tags.

What are head-jerking otters communicating? They could be greeting and identifying other individuals, conveying information about social status, or learning about the sex and reproductive condition of each otter. Much of this information is probably conveyed by the otter's well-developed sense of smell.

Perhaps the most obvious way sea otters communicate involves vocalizing. Although otters may seem quiet to many people, it's just that most of the sounds they make are soft and difficult to hear from shore, except for the scream call emitted by mothers and pups. Otters produce at least ten different types of vocalizations, including screams, whimpers, squeaks, whines, whistles, coos, grunts, growls, snarls, and hisses.

Recordings of several male otters temporarily held together in an outdoor pen revealed that they loudly whistled, squeaked and squealed while eating, interacting and playing. Grunting or cooing sounds are heard when otters are eating, especially if the food's particularly tasty. When captured, otters often growl, squeal or hiss. Frustrated or mildly distressed otters may whine or whistle. Older pups often whine when their mothers don't allow them to suckle. Some adult males attempting to mate with uncooperative females emit a plaintive call similar to the whine of a dog begging for a bone. Pair-bonded males and females exchange soft cooing sounds during their courtship. Mother-pup pairs also coo.

Pups are the noisiest otters. When a mother leaves her pup to forage for food, the pup often squeals in a high-pitched "wee wee" call, like the cry of a gull. A pup calling to its mother may be saying, "Where are you?" or "Feed me!" Screams directed toward an adult male may mean, "Leave my mother and me alone." Mothers vocalize less often than pups, but do emit loud calls to locate or maintain contact with their offspring. Each female's call seems to sound different, and analyses of recordings reveal quite a bit of individual variation in their vocalizations. The call of one Monterey mother sounds like a raspy quacking duck, while another cries in an earsplitting high-pitched scream. These unique "voiceprints" probably help mother and pup find and recognize each other if separated.

An otter entering a raft of otters may wake up the resting otters by "head jerking" or nuzzling or pouncing on them. Otters appear to communicate with each other by means of scent, vocalization and behavior.

7

Mating and Giving Birth

Female "Rudolph" was named for her bright red and terribly swollen nose that researchers could identify her with for weeks. You couldn't help feeling sorry for poor Rudolph, who had obviously been through a recent and intense bout of mating. While most females don't get such severe nose injuries, a female with a red swollen nose has almost certainly just mated. A female's nose serves as a good "handle" for a male to grasp with his teeth, as he wraps his forelegs around her chest and tries to hold on to the slippery female. As a result, a female's nose is often permanently scarred. Amazingly, Rudolph's severely damaged nose healed so well that observers could no longer identify her a few weeks later. Males appear to differ in their mating styles and some, like Nosebuster, seem consistently rougher on females' noses than other males. Many bright red noses decorated Nosebuster's territory.

Along the California coast you may see mating throughout the year. Sea otters appear to have a serially polygamous mating system in which an otter male mates with more than one partner, but only with one at a time over a period of days. A territorial male mates or forms a pair-bond with several different females at various times throughout the year. A female often mates with only one male during the brief time she ovulates and is sexually receptive, a period called estrus. However, a number of females have mated or pair-bonded with two or even three different males when in estrus.

Female California sea otters tend to reach sexual maturity when they're three to five years old, although researchers have seen females mate that are only two years old. Josephine, a female followed by researchers since she was born, mated for the first time at two years and gave birth six months later, but her pup died soon after birth.

A female comes into estrus and mates immediately after she weans her pup. But what happens if a female's pup dies, like Josephine's, or is lost before weaning? Aquarium researchers followed many Monterey females that lost very young pups and found that they mated again within about one month, ensuring that they would give birth again a few months later, but the period between pup loss and mating was longer than that of the females that successfully weaned their pups. Observations of aged females suggest that they may go through an additional estrus cycle or will continue to mate or pair-bond with various males for several weeks, almost as if they have trouble conceiving or miscarry soon after conception.

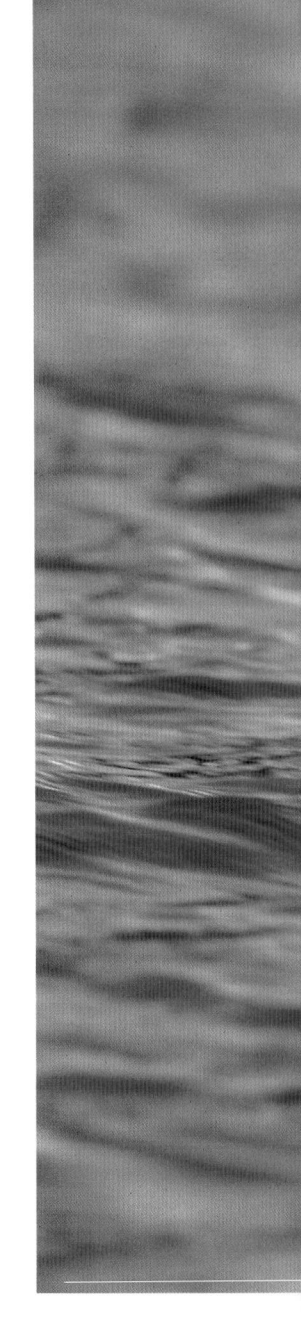

Most females receive nose injuries when males grip their snouts during mating. Wounds may be minor or severe, but usually result in pink nose scars which help researchers identify individuals.

A male and a receptive female often form a brief pair-bond, yet this bond isn't always necessary for mating to occur. The pair-bond often lasts about three to four days, but the male and female may stay together for only one day, or for as long as ten days. The mated pair remains close at all times—feeding, grooming and resting together. Only mother-pup pairs rest side-by-side as closely as mated pairs.

The male keeps close tabs on his female's whereabouts, at times remaining practically glued to her side as she swims and dives for food. Sometimes a male steals his mate's food as they feed together. You might also see a male engage in a courtship behavior informally known as "yo-yo bumping." The male, appearing to be attached to the female by an invisible string, repeatedly swims back and forth by his resting mate, bumping her with his back during each pass. Sometimes the female ignores this endless prodding, while at other times she'll stop resting and engage in mating activity—perhaps to put a stop to the incessant bumping, which can go for 20 minutes at a time!

It's fairly easy to mistake nonsexual play for mating, since both involve a lot of mutual nuzzling, pawing and rolling together. Real copulation between two otters, however, is definitely not playful and can get a bit rough at times. The male grasps the female's face or nose with his teeth while the pair roll and splash about on the surface. The female assumes a distinctive belly-up position with her head bent backward toward the water, with the male beneath her. Copulation typically lasts for 15 to 30 minutes and always takes place in the water.

Biologists believe that a female is sexually receptive for only a few days, ending after her pair-bond association with a male if she becomes pregnant. It's to a male's advantage to form a pair-bond

When sea otters mate, the male grasps the female with his claws and bites her nose as she lies on top of him, head bent back.

In Monterey Bay, the Lovers Point male #212 held the same territory between Lovers Point and Hopkins Marine Station for eleven years. Adult males maintain territories along roughly half-mile sections of coastline and constantly patrol their boundaries, checking out any females resting within their turf.

with a female in estrus, since the female cannot copulate with another male while she's so closely guarded by her mate. Exclusive and repeated copulations by the pair-bonded male ensure that he sires that female's offspring.

Territories Adult male California sea otters establish and maintain territories in female areas both seasonally and throughout the year. It isn't easy for a male to secure a good territory. Although males may become sexually mature when they're about five years old, they probably can't hold a territory until they're eight to ten years old. What's prime territory for an otter? A good site has an abundance of giant kelp, plenty of sheltered areas for resting and a good food supply—all qualities that attract females.

Researchers have studied territorial males in the Monterey Bay and San Simeon areas for several years. Along the coast from the Monterey Harbor to Point Pinos, nine or ten male territories border each other, spaced roughly a half-mile apart. Southern males off San Simeon abandon their territories in the winter and spring season when there appear to be fewer sexually receptive females in this area. Yet the northern males off Monterey remain in their territories throughout the year, perhaps because the kelp canopies persist longer along the more protected northern Monterey peninsula. It's also likely that more estrous females are available throughout the year in Monterey.

In both the northern and southern areas, males return to the same territory year after year. The older males off Hopkins Marine Station and Lovers Point have held the same territories for 10 and

11 years, respectively. Males constantly patrol the boundaries of their territories, swimming rapidly and intently on their bellies. They sometimes advertise their presence with especially energetic and highly visible splashing, kicking and grooming—perhaps warning other males to stay away. Only females and pups, and occasionally, recently weaned juvenile males, can rest within a male's territory. Adult males just passing through may be permitted to swim through the area uncontested.

Outright fighting among males for territorial rights or for mates is rare. When a fight does occur, the two males rise high up out of the water, pushing, shoving and lunging at each other. These deadly serious interactions exhibit none of the typical otter playfulness about them. Sometimes you'll see nasty bite wounds on a male's face and hindflippers, most likely inflicted during a fight.

Pregnancy Sea otters have a relatively long pregnancy, or gestation period, of six-and-a-half months, although gestation length varies widely from about four- to eight-and-a-half months. The long gestation allows the pup to develop as fully as possible inside the mother's womb before being born into the cold ocean. After a female conceives, implantation and further development of the embryo often stops for a while, postponing the pup's birth. This remarkable, but rather mysterious, phenomenon, called "delayed implantation," may be an adaptation that allows birth to coincide with favorable environmental conditions, or when the mother is in good physical condition. While the extent of the delay isn't well known, it seems to be relatively brief among many California otters, and may vary considerably. Delayed implantation also occurs in other mustelids and in seals.

Birth Few people have ever seen a female sea otter give birth. Births occur throughout the year in Monterey Bay, although it's possible that pupping may be more seasonal along the more exposed coast in the southern part of the range. California females may give birth either in the water or on land. For several days following birth, mothers with newborn pups often rest apart from other otters. Newborn pups aren't much bigger than a large kitten and weigh only about three to five pounds. A newborn looks somewhat like a

A young pup often rides on its mother's chest, left. A mother sea otter, right, may grab her pup's neck fur in her mouth and tow it along as she swims, especially if the pup has been "misbehaving."

floppy rag doll as the mother holds it high above the water while licking and grooming its fluffy fur. Young pups have a very light brownish or yellowish fur called the "natal pelage," which gives them an almost porcupinelike appearance. This fluffy fur helps a pup stay afloat on the surface, and is completely replaced by sleek, dark-brown adult fur when the pup's about three months old.

Unlike river otters that bear their young in litters, sea otters almost always give birth to single pups, as do other marine mammals. Although sea otters produce twins on rare occasions, a female can't adequately care for both pups and abandons one of the twins. Even though sea otters produce only one pup at a time, a California female living to 16 years of age and giving birth each year could have as many as 12 pups in her lifetime, making her a great-great-grandmother.

Generally, a female California sea otter gives birth every year and cares for her pup for about five-and-a-half months, although there is a great deal of individual as well as geographical variation in this reproductive cycle. In a few areas of Alaska, females appear to give birth every two years and care for their pup for one year or longer, whereas in other areas, the length of pup dependency period and reproductive cycle are similar to that found in California. There is a remarkable variation in the length of pup dependency periods, which range from four to nine months in California and two to 11 months in Prince William Sound.

Well-meaning rescuers should not pick up wild orphan pups, but should call local wildlife agencies and observe the pup to see if its mother is nearby.

Caring for Orphans

A dedicated group of volunteer caretakers, supervised by Monterey Bay Aquarium husbandry staff, provides the round-the-clock care needed by orphaned newborn pups. These caretakers groom each pup to keep its fur clean and dry, fluff-drying the thick fur, then brushing it with a variety of combs and brushes.

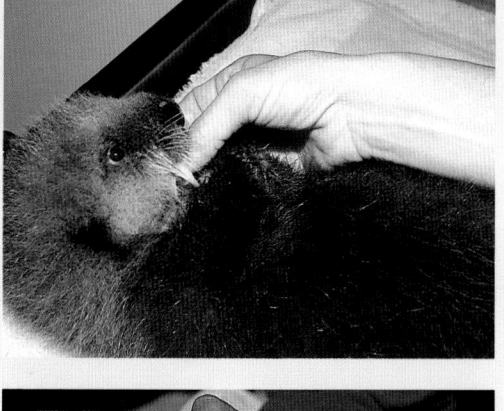

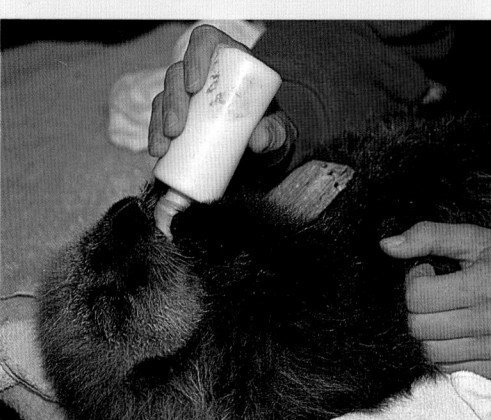

When the orphan pups are young, their caretakers use bottles fitted with latex nipples to feed them a blended formula of clams, squid, cod liver oil, half-and-half, fluids to prevent dehydration, vitamins and minerals. At approximately one month of age, the orphans begin eating small pieces of solid food.

A peek into the pups' indoor nursery reveals a waterbed for sleeping, a saltwater pool for "swimming lessons," and a large supply of toys for chewing, playing, and the development of motor skills. As the pups grow older, they begin spending more time outdoors in an 18-foot circular holding pool—filled with kelp and live prey—or in the aquarium's Great Tide Pool. A haul-out platform is sometimes placed inside the tank so younger pups can haul out of the water. The platform is removed when they get older to help them get used to sleeping in the water.

The demise of the waterbed as sleeping quarters for one young otter occurred when the six-month-old pup chewed on the mattress with her sharp teeth. According to a caretaker, "When I walked in that morning, the floor was soaking wet and the only visible part of the pup was her rear end sticking out of the waterbed. She'd bitten a big hole in the bed and was on her way inside to check it out. That day, we decided she had outgrown the waterbed." Husbandry staff have found that as pups mature they prefer to spend more time in the water. Now orphaned pups leave the waterbed for their outdoor home when they're about three months old. A hammocklike rubber mat, partially submerged in the saltwater pool, is also being used to transition pups into the water. This device supports the pup while it rests partially submerged in saltwater—much as it would rest on its mother's stomach.

Orphaned pups get round-the-clock care at the aquarium, where a dedicated crew of caretakers feed, clean, groom and play with them.

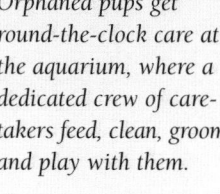

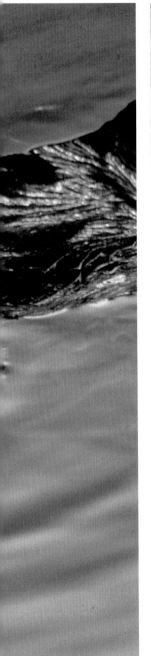

Mothers and Pups

The relationship between a mother and her pup represents the most enduring and intimate association in a sea otter's life. Adult males provide no parental care, which is typical for most mammals. A female sea otter is very solicitous of her pup. She invests a great deal of time and energy in caring for her offspring, which depends on her for nourishment, grooming and protection, especially when it's very young.

A mother and her pup are never far apart during the entire time the female cares for her young. A pup spends most of its time riding on its mother's belly. Even very large pups, six months or older, may still try to "climb on board." You can't help but feel sorry for a mother struggling to paddle with a pup nearly her own size riding on her stomach!

A mother's protective behavior toward her offspring is obvious to even the most casual observer. She may actually continue to carry her pup for several days after it has died, even attempting to groom the carcass. In Monterey Harbor, one female who'd just lost her pup was seen "mothering" a beer bottle—holding it under her chin and manipulating it as if it were a pup. When a pup is captured during tagging operations, the mother always remains near the boat, circling, calling, and clearly placing herself at risk. One unusually brave mother actually climbed into the boat to rescue her large pup, which

Mothers care for their
offspring for about six
months, although the
dependency period
varies among otters.
    The huge pup sinking
its mother, left, is close
to weaning age but is
still trying to suckle.

A mother often grooms her pup while it nurses. Sea otter milk is extremely rich, containing 20 to 25 percent fat.

was being tagged by biologists. Fortunately, startled researchers restrained the female—later named "Supermom,"—before she could chase them overboard.

While attentive to their own young, females rarely care for another mother's pup, probably in part because there's little chance that a mother who has lost her own pup will encounter an orphan. Aquarium researchers observed one interesting case of pup adoption by an old adult female they had been studying. Female #203 apparently had just lost her own pup when she came across a large female pup that had recently lost her own mother. Female #203 cared for this orphan for two to three weeks—nursing the pup, sharing food with her and protecting her from harm. Eventually, however, she abandoned the orphan, which was found dead on a nearby beach a few days later.

Fat-rich Milk A pup gets most of its nourishment by nursing from its mother for the first two months of its life. Although a mother continues to suckle her pup throughout the dependency period, the pup gradually adds more solid food to its diet. A female's two nipples are often visible on her lower abdomen when she's producing milk. Like other marine mammals, sea otters produce milk that's extremely rich in fat and protein and low in lactose or milk sugar. About 20 to 25 percent of sea otter milk is made up of fat. Seal and whale milk is even richer, sometimes containing as much as 50 percent fat. By comparison, cow's milk and human milk contain only about three to four percent fat and one to three percent protein. Even the richest ice cream contains only about 15 percent fat. The rich fat and protein content of sea otter milk provides a high-energy diet that promotes rapid tissue growth, crucial for survival in a marine environment.

Learning Otter Skills   While still with its mother, a pup gradually develops the skills it needs to survive on its own. Like human
babies, the rate of development of various skills seems to vary from
pup to pup. A pup first tries to groom itself when it's about three-
and-a-half weeks old, although it doesn't become really proficient at
grooming until about two months later.

A pup begins to swim to its mother about one month after birth.
Unable to swim on its back as well as an adult until it's two months
old or so, a young pup swims belly-down by making uncoordinated
wriggling motions with its body and hindflippers. Despite the pup's
hard work, progress is slow, almost as though it's on a treadmill. By
the time it's three to four months, the pup swims and dives with ease.

Because of the special natal fur that keeps it extremely buoyant,
a pup can't dive very well for the first three months of its life. Pups
trying to dive simply bob back to the surface like furry corks. It's
rather like trying to dive under water while wearing a life preserver.
So instead of diving with its mother, a young pup sticks its head

This sleeping pup, left, couldn't sink if it wanted to. Pups are born with a natal fur that keeps them floating like corks.

Female #190, with her pup in Monterey Harbor, was well known to researchers who followed two of her pups, which lived in the same area after they were weaned.

under water, peering like a snorkeler at mom as she dives and forages below. By two-and-a-half months, a pup will follow its mother
on feeding dives. One month later, the pup can stay submerged as
long as an adult on an average one-minute dive.

Pups often capture inedible prey, like the straw in this youngster's mouth, until they learn the correct foods to eat.

   Throughout the dependency period, pups gradually learn the
complex foraging skills they will need later in life. By six months of
age, pups are able to capture and break open their own prey. However,
like all beginners, sea otter pups make many mistakes in the course
of learning how to forage. Young pups capture all sorts of inedible
objects, such as pieces of driftwood, broken shells, kelp, rocks, empty
bottles, golf balls and even old shoes. This motley assortment of
"prey" is repeatedly tasted, unsuccessfully pounded or abandoned.
Female #182's pup wasn't too popular with Hopkins Marine Station
researchers after he repeatedly "captured" and completely shredded
a large styrofoam buoy marking a study site. Pups apparently have
a sizeable array of junk to choose from in areas heavily used by
people, like the Monterey Harbor. One pup feeding in the harbor
collected a varied assortment of trash while foraging, finally surfac-
ing with a large automobile tire!

   When a pup does capture real prey, however, it doesn't always
know what to do with its live meal, and may spend a great deal of
time dealing with pinching crab claws and squirming octopus tentacles, or trying to break open a hard shell. Researchers have found
that a pup will often discard difficult-to-open prey and pester mom
until she hands over a pre-shelled and ready-to-chew piece of crab
or snail. How desirable can a sharp-spined urchin seem to a pup
who can't get inside to the tasty part? Pups can't use rock tools very
efficiently to break open prickly or hard-shelled prey until they're
five or six months old.

Badgering Mom As pups grow older, their constant demands for food and attention must become quite a nuisance. Large pups take advantage of their mothers as much as possible, stealing food, attempting to nurse or hitching a ride at every opportunity. By the age of two-and-a-half months, a pup usually "asks for" and receives food each time its mother surfaces with prey. Even five- to six-month-old pups generally allow their mothers to do most of their foraging for them. One six-month-old pup, perfectly capable of finding its own food, lazily watched his mother, "No-nose," dive for food. He'd take some only when she'd capture abalone—his apparent favorite. Another pup excitedly pounced on its mother whenever she surfaced with snails, which it evidently preferred. Many pups seem to find *Pisaster* sea stars particularly distasteful, and will promptly toss away any sea stars mom tries to pass their way. It may be that pups dislike the sea star's sticky tube feet that cling to their fur. Once a human surrogate mother gave an orphaned otter pup a sea star that promptly stuck tight to his shoulder. The pup frantically zoomed around the kelp trying to dislodge the sticky star until his surrogate mom managed to remove the offending prey.

Although a mother often offers her pup some or all of her prey, many larger pups constantly steal food from their mothers, at times snatching snacks directly out of their mouths! Pups also try neck-squeezing and head-bopping their mothers to swipe prey. Perhaps to ensure that she gets something to eat, a mother sometimes rapidly stuffs food in her own mouth or stores some for herself in her underarm pouches while giving her pup something else to chew on.

Mothers are extremely tolerant of such harassment, although they may snap at their frisky offspring or try to avoid their pups. A mother with an older pup that's persistently trying to nurse sometimes slowly rotates and twirls in the water or swims belly-down, trying to dislodge the pup and end unnecessary nursing. If a pup remains firmly attached to its mother's nipple, even under water, a quick and violent twist usually dislodges the youngster. Perhaps the pup's insistent behavior makes it easier for its mother to wean her demanding offspring when the time comes.

Pups will attempt to get handouts from mom long after they can forage for themselves. This pup is soliciting pelagic red crab from its mother.

Sea Otter Rehabilitation

Since 1984, Monterey Bay Aquarium staff have been developing a rehabilitation program for stranded otters. The goal is to return stranded sea otters back to their natural home. Older pups and juveniles that have been cared for by their mothers appear to have a good chance of surviving as wild otters. Younger pups that haven't had the benefit of interacting with their mothers for long often don't have the skills needed to survive in the wild. Rehabilitation staff try to help these young animals acquire these skills without letting the pups imprint on them. Despite the best attempts of aquarium staff, some sea otters do bond with the people who care for them, and as a result have trouble adjusting to life in the wild.

One such orphan was Roscoe, a tiny two-week-old male pup stranded on Del Monte Beach on March 26, 1986. Because the aquarium had no exhibit space for Roscoe, he was discouraged from bonding to people as he grew older. Roscoe spent most of his time in an outdoor tank and was given live food, such as crabs, snails, mussels and clams, to prepare him for foraging in the wild. When he was about eight months old, aquarium staff released Roscoe into Monterey Bay by way of the aquarium's Great Tide Pool. Researchers closely monitored his progress.

During his first two days of freedom, Roscoe remained in the Great Tide Pool, swimming, whining loudly, and eating food provided every few hours by staff who were helping him through his transition to self-sufficiency. Roscoe even managed to climb the steep concrete stairs to the deck, where he stubbornly sat and cried in front of a crowd of sympathetic visitors.

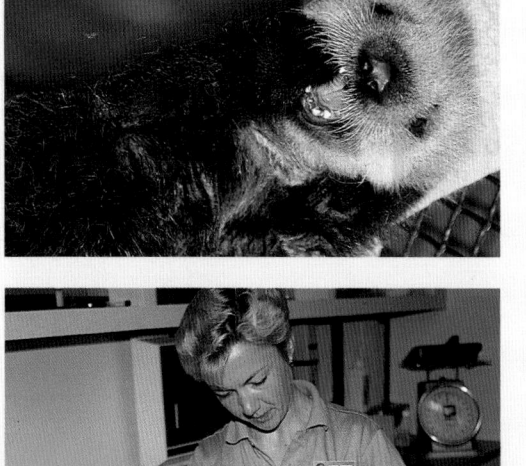

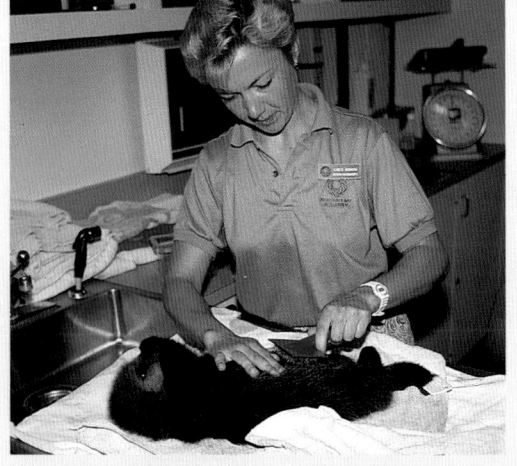

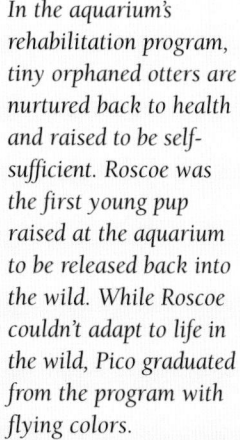

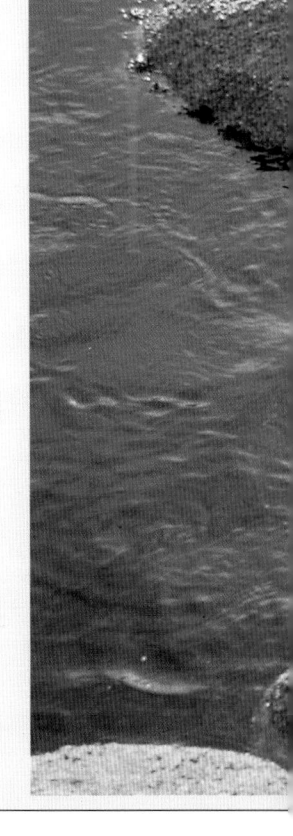

In the aquarium's rehabilitation program, tiny orphaned otters are nurtured back to health and raised to be self-sufficient. Roscoe was the first young pup raised at the aquarium to be released back into the wild. While Roscoe couldn't adapt to life in the wild, Pico graduated from the program with flying colors.

At one point, a visitor accidentally dropped his expensive camera into the Great Tide Pool near Roscoe. The tourist's initial relief that his camera had landed on a dry spot quickly turned to dismay when Roscoe snatched it and began pounding it, like any other otter rock tool, against the concrete ledge.

Roscoe finally ventured away from the aquarium and swam into Monterey Harbor where he began jumping into small boats and approaching people—one of whom coincidentally happened to be one of his former caretakers. After six days of freedom, a tired, skinny Roscoe beached himself at Cypress Point in Pebble Beach. He had not been able to find enough food in the wild and had imprinted so strongly on his caretakers that he couldn't adapt to life as a wild otter.

Roscoe's story ended happily, however. Due to the unfortunate loss of one of the exhibit otters in August 1986, there was now room for him as a permanent resident in the aquarium. Jiggs, a male otter on exhibit, suffered from a twisted intestine and died a few hours after surgery. Roscoe took Jiggs' place, and quickly adjusted to his new home. For the most part, the female exhibit otters readily accepted Roscoe, who appears quite content with his status as sole male among the all-female group.

Many orphaned pups have participated in the aquarium's rehabilitation program with variable success. Some have survived, learning how to groom themselves, find food and interact with wild otters. Others couldn't adapt to life as wild otters, and while a few died, most were returned to captivity and now live at other aquariums and zoos where they inspire interest in their species among people that live far from the coast.

Pup Survival in California and Alaska

Recent research has revealed a disturbingly high rate of mortality among California sea otter pups. As many as 40 percent die before reaching a minimum weaning age of four months. Most of these pups are lost within a month of birth. And more young otters probably don't make it after they are weaned and on their own.

This high loss of pups, which does not occur in Alaska, is probably one of the main reasons that the California otter population has grown so slowly in comparison to northern populations. In Alaska, for example, the average rate of pup loss is only 15 percent at Kodiak Island and 13 to 25 percent in Prince William Sound. Alaskan pups are able to survive on their own at a younger age than California pups. Pups as young as two or three months are weaned successfully in Alaska. At weaning, Alaskan pups also weigh more—between 35 and 44 pounds—than California pups, which average 24 to 31 pounds. In California, we know of several pups that managed to survive, even to adulthood, after leaving their mothers at the age of four to five months. But most are cared for by their mothers for nearly six months, and some offspring are seven to nine months old before they leave their mothers.

Why do so many pups die in California? Why are Alaskan pups younger and heavier when weaned? Scientists don't yet know the answers, but speculate that possible reasons include differences between the two areas in weather and sea conditions and type of available habitat, or perhaps the effects of environmental contaminants, diseases and parasites on females in California. It's possible that central California does not offer ideal habitat in which to raise a pup compared with more northern areas closer to the center of the sea otters' natural range. For instance, Prince William Sound provides a diversity of habitats to sea otters in comparison with more uniform habitat available along the California coast. Otters in Prince William Sound may travel among the different habitat patches to meet their needs and those of their pups, moving to more sheltered areas during storms or shallow-water mussel beds where older pups can forage more easily.

This California sea otter mother carries her fuzzy, young pup on her belly. Older mothers seem to lose fewer pups in the first few months after birth.

Alaskan sea otters, like this one hauled out on the ice, have larger pups and higher success rates in raising their young past weaning age than California sea otters.

Research focusing on the possible causes of such high pup mortality among southern otters should enhance the recovery and conservation of the California population.

We have learned, however, that older sea otter mothers in California are more likely to wean pups successfully than younger mothers—a pattern found in other mammals and birds as well. Pup mortality rates are 60 percent for three- to six-year-old otter mothers, 25 percent for seven- to ten-year-old mothers, and zero for 11- to 14-year-old mothers.

More parenting experience may help the older otter mothers successfully raise their pups. Competent mothering abilities are especially valuable among species like the sea otter in which the female produces only a limited number of offspring throughout her lifetime, and the young require a prolonged or intensive period of parental care. Maternal care in sea otters is relatively long and appears to involve complex mothering skills, such as grooming, nursing, feeding and protecting the pup, as well as the mother's ability to find enough food for herself and her offspring. Mothers must give their pups over one-quarter of all the food they capture, on average, and some females share nearly half of their prey with their pups. Mistakes made in mothering due to lack of experience may be costly, and older sea otter mothers are probably better sea otter mothers in more cases than not.

9

Growing Up

How does a mother wean her pup? What happens to pups after they're weaned? We don't have all the answers yet, but we're beginning to understand the nature of the weaning process, where newly weaned pups and juvenile otters go, what they eat and how they behave socially.

A mother often appears to travel at weaning time. Two females, for instance, stayed in Monterey Harbor with their pups for months, but immediately left and moved a couple of miles away at weaning time. Two other females traveled all the way to Santa Cruz when weaning their pups. Sexual interactions between a mother and an adult male who senses she's approaching estrus may prompt mothers and pups to separate, or at least play a role in the weaning process. Or the demands of a nearly full-grown offspring may become so draining that the mother can't continue to care for her pup without endangering her own health. Severe storms and rough sea conditions also seem to promote mother and pup separations, and, at times, premature weaning.

Pups weigh approximately 25 to 30 pounds at weaning, 15 to 20 pounds less than an average adult female. You can often tell juveniles from full-grown adults by their smaller size, darker brown fur and puplike behavior. Young otters often dive with a distinctive jerky flip of the tail and hindflippers, as though they haven't quite mastered the art of the smooth "tuck" foraging dive.

Juveniles are also more playful than adults. Young adolescent males spend much of their "free" time playing and rough-housing in boisterous bachelor groups. Juvenile females sometimes play with such enticing toys as discarded plastic bags, old socks or styrofoam cups—things they find floating on the surface or littering the bottom.

Two-year-old female #557 became intrigued with a large plastic tube that fit snugly over her head. She spent quite a while diving and cavorting with her "plastic mask," which at one point became stuck on her head! After a few minutes of concerted tugging, however, she managed to remove the offending tube. She's since been called by the affectionate, although somewhat undignified, name of Tubehead.

Where do pups go after they're weaned? Juvenile males tend to disperse a greater distance from their birth area than females. Most juvenile males leave home soon after weaning. They're probably booted out of these female areas by adult territorial males. Some young males travel extensively; one recently weaned male near Big Sur

Juvenile sea otters are smaller, often have darker fur and behave more like pups than adult otters.

An adult male otter keeps close tabs on a female who's about to wean her pup, and will soon be ready to mate.

traveled up and down the California range, covering hundreds of miles in several weeks! Many of these young males eventually join male groups at either end of the range. Researchers also find large numbers of juvenile males quite a distance from shore, where they forage and rest. Juvenile males may take up residence nearly two miles from shore.

In contrast, newly independent females often seem to remain within several miles of where they were born. A number of tagged adult females born and raised in Monterey Bay have lived in the same area since the late 1970s, and many have given birth to their own pups. A few of these older females live in the same vicinity as their daughters and granddaughters. So there seems to be some degree of matrilineal kin relationships among the local otters, as well as opportunities for mothers and daughters to interact.

Juvenile pups sometimes hang onto buoys in the harbor when they rest, or may drape rope over themselves instead of kelp.

*Mischievous juveniles
and pups love to play,
whether on a diver's
inflatable raft, top, with
a rope on a pier, above,
or by climbing on a
plywood "raft" with a
bull kelp stipe for a
rudder, left.*

Most of the recently weaned juvenile females seem to move around quite a bit, although they don't travel nearly as far as juvenile males. Young females may rest and forage near the center of their birth area for a few weeks, but at other times remain on the "outskirts of town" where fewer adults live. Researchers have seen these juvenile females, who maybe haven't yet kicked the milk habit, trying to suckle from apparently unrelated adult females. These older females, who probably aren't producing milk anyway, usually tolerate this inappropriate behavior for awhile, but may snap at the juvenile if she persists in her milk-stealing attempts.

The huge "pup" on the right dwarfs its mother as it solicits a handout.

Family Reunions Do mothers ever associate with their former offspring? From what researchers know so far, reunions occasionally occur. Yet continued study of tagged mothers and their weaned offspring may show that these sorts of interactions, while difficult to observe, are more common than previously thought. In a number of cases, researchers have seen females and their former pups together when the offspring were as young as a few months old, or as old as several years. Sometimes mother and daughter seemed to ignore each other, yet in most cases, they interacted in some way.

A two-year-old daughter, Josephine, behaved very nervously around her mother, #190, who snapped at her daughter a couple of times when she nosed her mother's belly. Josephine seemed to want to stay near her mother, yet at the same time she was very respectful and a little leery of her. A few months later, Josephine and her mother tumbled and rolled together, but this time #190 had a new pup. Another mother and her adult daughter were seen nuzzling each other and briefly interacting in a "social" and nonaggressive way.

Other longer-lasting mother-pup reunions have taken place. A juvenile female otter, who was apparently weaned, was captured, tagged and moved to another location about three miles away in Monterey. Yet three days later, observers saw this same female being nursed and groomed by her mother back at the capture site! In Alaska, a researcher kept records on a one-year-old female who rejoined her mother after they'd been separated through the winter. The mother didn't have another pup yet, and the daughter remained with her for another four months, enjoying quite a few "free" meals.

Another reunion took place between female #184 and her eight-month-old daughter, #535. Ten days after weaning her pup and mating, female #184 reunited with her daughter for nearly two more months. The mother continued to groom her pup, offering her food and holding her while sleeping. When first reunited, however, female #184 usually pushed #535 away with her hindflippers when she attempted to nurse, no matter how loudly her offspring squealed. Once pup #535 persistently tried to suckle after being pushed away 25 times in a row! After the second weaning, female #184 mated again. She cared for her pup for just over nine months—an exceptionally long dependency period for a California sea otter.

After being weaned, pup #535 spent some time feeding and swimming in the same area as her mother. Pup #535 also ate kelp crabs, purple urchins and mussels, just like her mother. She tended to feed on very small-sized prey, including tiny kelp crabs no bigger than a fingernail. When she was just over four years old, female #535 gave birth to her first pup. The last we knew, she still lived in the same area, ate the same foods, and even hauled out among the same rocks as her mother did when #535 was a pup.

The Future of Otters   Much more probably goes on in sea otter society than researchers currently understand, as these and other detailed observations of individuals like #535 and her mother are beginning to reveal. We still have a great deal to learn about these fascinating marine mammals. Yet the sea otter population in California remains small and vulnerable—a fragile evolutionary link with the ancient otters that once flourished along the shores of California long before the appearance of our own ancestors. As long as we protect the California otter population, sea otters will continue to provide us with a marvelous source of scientific discovery, education and entertainment for many decades to come. With hope and hard work, current protection efforts will succeed, and our children and grandchildren will be able to share our fascination with the playful and captivating California sea otter.

Sea otters, which remain extremely vulnerable in a human world, rely on our protection for their continued survival.

Index